THE LOSER LETTERS

A Comic Tale of Life, Death,
and Atheism

by
Mary Eberstadt

IGNATIUS PRESS   SAN FRANCISCO

Previously published material is
used by permission of *National Review*

Cover art:

Front cover photo © istockphoto/PeJo29

Cover design by Roxanne Mei Lum

ISBN 978-1-58617-431-6
Library of Congress Control Number 2009935087
Printed in the United States of America ⊗

For Nick

CONTENTS

FOREWORD

An open letter to those spokesmen for the new Atheism who have labored mightily these last few years to sweep aside religion's paralytic webs of superstition and prejudice, and to liberate the rest of our Species via Science and Enlightenment:

Dear Sirs,

Speaking just for *this* Atheist convert, congratulations, guys—You really did it! Thanks to all Your hard work, the rest of us know once and for all that the so-called "God", that Loser, is everything You say he is: the biggest fraud of all time, cosmic zero, ultimate no-show—and after all those centuries and promises too. It's like throwing the biggest rave ever, only to cancel at the last minute after everyone'd already bought tickets and drugs for it. What kind of deity does that, anyway? If this were Facebook, no one would be friending him now.

But You have to admit: that same Loser sure has been great for the book business—including and especially all those books on the new Atheism, I'm happy to say. Almost a million volumes sold in twelve months' time; covers in every major newspaper and magazine; publicity on all the best talk shows and Web sites and campuses; national and international book awards up the wazoo—talk about knowing how to make "something" ($$$) out of "nothing" (Loser)!

It really is marvelous—sorry; I almost said "miraculous" there (I'm new to the Atheist party and hope You'll pardon any slips)—how Your ideas have taken so much of the Western media by storm. You'd almost think Atheism had friends in some pretty high places! Whatever, You probably think we Atheists have earned the right to sit back and chill. I mean, it's pretty clear we've won by now—isn't it?

Except, well, maybe not—and that's why I'm writing You this letter. Because there's one thing that's still missing from Atheism's final victory, and it's something that just can't be sugarcoated. Ahem: apart from me, where is the testimony of anyone Your writings have actually convinced? After all, as one of You said somewhere and all of us want to believe, "If this book works as I intend, religious readers will be Atheists when they put it down." So where are the rest of them, I'm starting to wonder—these other converts (like me!) to the new godlessness?

I'm not asking about the numbers to depress any of You. One of the things I love about our side—the winning side, the *Atheist* side!—is we get that it's good enough just being in everybody's face about "God" not existing, even if no one but me was persuaded *despite* a few million more books in circulation. And I know that it wouldn't be the first time that Atheism fell short on the convert count. "It appears to me (whether rightly or wrongly)", as our most illustrious Forebear Charles Darwin once put it, "that direct arguments against Christianity and theism produce hardly any effect on the public." And He should certainly know!

Even so, as Your convert, in fact as maybe Your one and only convert, I worry for us. Sooner or later, one of the believers will come along and point out a fact he'll think is damaging to this new Atheism—I mean, that it hasn't actually convinced anyone. In other words, he's going to paint our side as somehow intellectually unfit. And the idea of being called unfit, to this newly minted Atheist, is just too much to bear. Back when I was a Christian, I was taught to embrace those kind of people—You know what I mean, the maladaptives. But as an Atheist, even a new one, I've learned to despise them all as Nature's mistakes. Being put on the losing side would be what You might call a personal devolution for me, something gross and unnatural—like having an opposable thumb and not even texting with it!

And so, to protect us Atheists from that charge before our religious enemies even get to it, I've decided to write the following Letters to You. They offer up the earnest confession of one who—as someone once said of our fellow Atheist Allen Ginsberg—"did not come back from Hell empty-handed." I mean Hell figuratively, of course! Little joke there! But seriously, I've ascended from the darkness of the believers by clinging to each and every one of Your words—and I bring with me recent firsthand knowledge of them and their ways that I want to share with You.

About the reasons for my conversion to Atheism, I'll have lots more to say in what follows. But let me first thank some of You for introducing that amped word, "Brights", to describe our side. It's meant to distinguish the "vigorous" and "healthy" souls of Atheists, as one of You put it somewhere, from those of the believers (sorry on "souls" BTW). In these pages I want to take that logic of "Brights" to another level—because, of course, if there are Brights, then by necessity our adversaries, a.k.a. the Christians, must be known by the opposite descriptive, "Dulls". And so they will be in the Letters ahead.

In short, I offer to You my own conversion story— that of a former Christian who has adapted at last to Atheism. It's a personal tale, by the way, not a point-by-point engagement with all of Your arguments and themes. After all, I'm no theologian (and neither are any of You, of course!). But before getting into all that,

I'll start at the beginning: by explaining what kept me—and not only me, but a great many other potential converts for our side—away from Atheism for so long.

Above all, I want all my Letters to be *useful*. I've read what Marxist Leninist Atheists had to say, back before they all went to wherever all the Marxist Leninist Atheists went after 1989. And I have to confess, at times I really miss their verve! Don't You? Especially their sense of how the highest purpose is to be useful.

Well, I think the most useful thing I can do here is to show You something of how the Dulls really think from the inside, so You can see what we're truly up against in trying to convert them. Just think of me as Your own private *Project Runway* or *What Not to Wear*—someone who just wants us Atheists to be all we can be.

I do hope everyone reads my story of personal evolution through. After all, it's the only one You have, at least so far. But don't let the numbers bother You much. One down, and just a few billion more to go!

> Your huge fan,
> A. F. (A Former) Christian

LETTER ONE
The Trouble with Experience

Dear Sirs (again),

First, let's talk about something You Atheist guys all like to talk about (judging by those latest books especially!), which is sex and the role that it plays in separating the benighted believers from the enlightened rest of us.

As I get it, our Atheist position on sex boils down to this: the believers with their tard regulations are all wrong about it, while we Brights have been—I'm reaching here for the words that You guys might use—so groovy and hip by throwing out the Christian rule book on all that stuff. Or to put it another way: thanks to Atheism and Secularism, more generally, words and phrases like "privacy", "consenting adults", and "behind closed doors" are in; and ones like "monogamy", "self-restraint", and "staying together for the kids" are out. If there's anything we Brights are all on the same page about—and again, I've read all those pages of Yours pretty carefully!—it would seem to be this; am I right?

Now, as a fresh convert myself, who is in a more or less delirious state at all times just *thinking* about what my new Atheism will mean for my personal life now that I've been freed from all those commandments, I'm certainly not here to argue with You about the appeal of doing what comes Naturally. At the same time, though, I have to warn You about something. A lot of what the new Atheism says about sex strikes me as strategically dangerous to us—the kind of talk that runs the risk of turning off some of the very believers, *especially* the younger believers, who might otherwise be tempted to switch over to our side.

Let's start with that generational difference between You new Atheists and some of the rest of us. Did Your parents ever leave home for the weekend when any of You were kids, putting You in the care of teenage siblings? Do You still remember the two-day nonstop party, and the expressions on Your parents' faces Sunday night when they saw the overflowing ashtrays and empty kegs and someone else's clothes in the laundry and throw-up in the fish tank? Well, You should know that's pretty much what it was like for those of us who went through life *after* You baby boomers did, a decade or so after what might be called the godless generation swept through first.

16

And this brings us to why Atheists run the risk of losing among this younger generation when You talk about sex the way new Atheists all have so far: because everybody on the godless team writes about sex and freedom from the religious moral rules as if all the years from 1960 on never even existed. As if the Sexual Revolution hadn't been staggering along for nearly a half century now! *Hello?* Well, for better or worse from the point of view of our side, it has. And what *that* means is that all kinds of people now know that if we try and make a selling point out of trashing Christian sexual morality—as Atheists have been doing since the beginning—a whole lot of Dulls today are going to raise their hands and call us *losers* again on the subject of sex and say that we don't know what we're talking about. So in this Letter I'd like to draw Your attention to just some of the legacy of the Sexual Revolution, in the hopes of making our Movement less vulnerable to the unfortunate facts.

We can begin where most Americans really begin to learn about sex, i.e., on the typical American campus of the past few decades. To live it is to see up close and personal that Dostoevsky's mantra—*when "God" is gone, everything is permitted*—is not some lame old literary prophecy, but a vibrating social fact. Of course, by saying "everything" is permitted on campus I don't literally mean *everything*, after all; these upper-middle-class

17

children, some still wearing braces and nearly all still depending on their doting parents for every library fine, have for the most part proved unlikely to take up mass murder or grand theft auto. But the part of "everything" that involves everybody's *favorite* something, i.e., risk-and-supposedly-consequence-free sex (or at least the promise thereof), has been different.

Looking back to my own years at the university, I'd say that if the place had had to choose a motto in English, likely the fittest would have been "Let copulation thrive!" if You know what I mean (and I bet You do!). And the connection between all this furtive fun behind doors and the absence of any public religiosity was quite obvious, at least to this former Christian. It wasn't just the deity who'd taken a hike off the quad, of course; authority in practically any form had disappeared along with Loser. But there's no doubt that "God" above all just wasn't done. In four years, I met one student who openly attended church, and the subsequent number I have uncovered were doing so more or less *samizdat*. That's what I'm trying to explain about this. The place was as pure as any Atheist's dream, as deity-free as the Bravo channel on Sunday morn (or any other time!).

Now why is any of this a problem for the Atheist side? Doy. First, the fact of what's been happening on campus all these years means that we Brights can't very well go around like the Communists always tried to, and say that the problem with our vision is that it "hasn't really been tried". No, Secularism/Atheism, when it comes to sexual mores anyway, *has* been tried, *is* being tried, and the empirical fact is that what's happening on campuses is what sex and "romance" look like when we Brights get our way and dispose of all those silly religious rules—two, three, many Charlotte Simmonses.

And if the campuses don't do it for You, take a look at what Secular sex is doing in post-Christian western Europe! Pornography is everywhere, over-the-counter medicines for STDs are front and center in every convenience store, red-light districts showcase poorer and younger people (mostly from the East) being paid for every possible combination of sex by richer and older people (mostly from the West), the age of consent keeps getting pushed lower—and marriage and children and families are disappearing.

Please don't misunderstand me here—I'm not saying it isn't all fantastic! I'm just saying something none of You mentioned when You talked about sex, which is that this is what things look like when we Atheists get our way.

See? That's Secularism for you; that's what it does. You can stand on your hind limbs like a proud biped and applaud it; you can pretend it is something other than what it is; you can say with a straight face that you're happy to send your own daughters into that kind of world, that you don't care how many men or women or even what Species she sleeps with—or what her partner devours for hours on end on the computer when she's asleep—as long as they are all somehow "responsible" about it; but that's pretty much the limit of what the facts will allow us to do.

What You can't do, any more than I could back in my Christian days, is to pretend that this atmosphere on campus, any more than the sterility of western Europe today, is somehow *accidental* to the absence of religious practice. Of course the two are glued together. Secularism is as Secularism does.

The second point I'd urge You all to consider—and, again, it's not the kind of thing guys of Your age might know, if You'll pardon my saying so—is that when we Atheists say with a straight face that deep-sixing the old sex rules will make everybody happy, we're dissing the experience of most people who have passed through college since the godless generation. I mean to say, that's pretty much everyone under the age of fifty. The Gen Xers on down have all seen firsthand the same things this former Christian did—that all this rutting and strutting and getting free contraceptives and living for the moment was not exactly the way Atheists all paint it in their books, i.e., as some fantastic liberation from the sexually repressive hand of the doddering Church.

Oh snap! In fact, and to the contrary, throwing out all the rules has actually been making a lot of people very miserable indeed—to say nothing of how miserable plenty of them were making *other* people. Maybe You somehow weren't around for all the hangovers and detoxing, the panicked trips to the shrinks and the clinics, the door slammings, and crying jags and suicide threats that so many of us think about when we think about college; but some of the rest of us saw enough to get pretty sick of all that and were tempted to think that a rule or two about how some members of the Species ought to treat others might not be all bad. It was mostly worse for the women than for the men, I'm thinking—which reminds me of something else that's the subject of a later Letter: You all *do* know some women, don't You?—but it wasn't so great for plenty of the guys, either.

So You see, one other reason for my own former resistance to Secularism and Atheism—and a big reason why many other believers resist us too—was just this: it seemed plain as the ring in my nose that the so-called Sexual Revolution, which is celebrated to a man (again, not a typo; more on that later too) by every Atheist, turned out not to be the benign bacchanal everyone said it would be; it was not the nonstop party of so many panting descriptions; it was not even the "Love Shack" of the B-52's; it was instead, from the point of

21

view of many of the believers, proof that Secular so-called morality once unleashed would do some real damage in the world.

I mean, even Christians can count on their fingers, You know, about things like the number of peers from broken homes who seemed to have "issues" that the ones from intact homes didn't; the number of girlfriends unhappy about their abortions, their sexually transmitted diseases, their inability to treat men as disposably as they were treated themselves; the number of men who turned out to make particularly crappy boyfriends because they'd been around the block one or ten or twenty too many times; the number of marriages split by the kinds of things consenting adults do when they're consenting with people outside of it—all just for instance.

Does any of this sound familiar? I'm sure it doesn't, because it's a part of sexual reality that Atheists never mention! But that's exactly why I'm harping on it. If our Movement is really going to go around arguing that the sooner we get rid of all those rules, the happier humanity is going to be, we're going to get blown away by this kind of counterevidence. It's enough to make You envy Bertrand Russell and all the Atheists who came before us, isn't it? Who were able to paint a happy face around all those things that didn't exist yet? Well, unfortunately we in the twenty-first century can't pretend we don't know.

The third point is that it's another very bad fact for our side that if people actually *followed* Dull sexual teaching, this would be a better and happier world than one in which they did not. (Note that I'm not including myself in there! As St. Augustine *should* have said, "Make *them* good, God, not me!" But You have to admit, there's a lot to be said for having the *rest* of the Species play by the rules.) Even worse, it suggests to some of them that the Dulls are on to something with this notion of natural law. Of course we Atheists should call it unnatural law, since nothing could be more foreign to our biological imperatives! But the odd thing is, again, that if everyone lived under their unnatural law, an awful lot of people would seem to be better off than they are now— and this is even true of the most controversial teachings, the ones You all most enjoy snickering at.

For example, if You had asked me back in my Christian days questions like: Would those girls have been better off without those abortions? Or: Would those kids have been happier being raised by both biological parents? Or: Do guys who have already slept with a hundred women make worse boyfriends than those who haven't? Or:—hit me where I really used to live!— Which set of rules, Atheism's or religion's, would You want Your own hypothetical children to live by? I'd have said the answers to all those and more were no-brainers— no-brainers that made points for the religious side, that is. I'll confess a terrible weakness here and say that even now, after I've evolved so far, I still want to reach for the Xanax just thinking about an Atheist like any of You dating my hypothetical daughter—as opposed to, say, a nice, antiabortion, save-sex-for-marriage Christian. I know it's terribly unfit; but is that just me?

The bottom line is, after everything that's happened since the Sexual Revolution, I'm telling You that we Atheists really need to knock off all the happy talk about how fantabulously liberating sex is. *Privacy, privacy, privacy* is everybody's mantra—as if that word settles anything at all! It's messed up, isn't it, when You think of how otherwise puritanical our own times are, that the Church's notion of sexual discipline should seem so funny to so many people? After all, it's the only kind of discipline that's out of bounds! We all know that people who eat too much are pigs, people who drink too much are drunks, people who don't exercise are slobs and parasites on the body politic what with all their health costs, and people who smoke are just as disgusting as it's possible to be, like an old person crossed with a fat one wearing a fur coat and eating venison and cake at the same time or something—and the rest of us are all really put out at every single one of those kinds of people for being such slobs and so hard on our own eyes and wallets. You know?

Yet sex behind closed doors, just as the Dulls point out, has more serious consequences for the world than *any* of these other kinds of piggishness. It's those "private acts" outside of marriage that have sent illegitimacy soaring and put so many kids in the rough hands of Mom's rotating boyfriends. It's consenting adults who have turned AIDS and STDs into global health problems. All this is to say nothing of the consequences that are harder to measure of all those mature adults doing as they please "in private". And kids know all about those kinds of consequences, as You can see if You ever look at their music and movies and Facebook pages. There's a backlash out there that none of You seem to know about—one You might call *Ozzie and Harriet, come back—all is forgiven!* I would go even further, based on what I saw as a Dull, and say that this notion of sexual discipline and its importance is not only serious rather than unserious; it is also what pulls many of the Dulls into practicing or even turning to religion in the first place, because they feel somehow better about life when it's lived inside of those rules.

Please understand that I'm not criticizing here! Cheering for pornography and omnivorous sex and, by extension, broken homes and abused and screwed-up kids and all the rest of the Sexual Revolution's fallout may not be *everyone's* thing; but most of You new Atheist guys have definitely made it Yours. I respect all that!

I'm just saying for now that we shouldn't fool our-selves into thinking that the believers' sexual codes are an unmitigated bad on them and a plus for us, when most evidence suggests it's quite the other way around.

Meanwhile, while we're still on this subject of what does and doesn't work for us when it comes to bring-ing others around to godlessness, let me raise a related point that You've been indulging to our possible long-term detriment (though not just You; the Enlighten-ment started it!). That is the argument that Reason itself is also on the Atheist side. As I'll explain in the next Letter, that's one potato we really need to drop before somebody gets burned by it.

Yours pretty faithfully,
A. F. Christian

LETTER TWO
Some Little Contradictions
and How They Grew

Dear Atheist Sirs (again),

I hope that by now You've all gotten my first Letter and that everybody's had a chance to read it and think over my points and suggestions. It was about sex (!), so I figured You'd all get to it. I know from Your books how interested Atheists are in *that* subject! And no worries: You'll definitely be hearing more about You-know-what from me in the future, *especially* once we get to my own personal Atheist conversion story.

For now, though, this second Letter is about something else I think we really need to talk about if we Brights are ever going to get serious about pulling other people besides me away from Loser. One other big problem facing us is this: Atheists everywhere—not just all of You but all Atheists going way back into the very

27

beginning of our Evolutionary leap into godlessness—keep talking about how Reason and Logic are *totally* in our corner. And for reasons explained below, I think this kind of talk runs the risk of being very off-putting to certain other members of the Species—especially those who for whatever random reason have been exposed even a little to Reason and Logic.

I know; I was one.

It didn't start out that way. Like so many other Americans, I was what You might call a cradle Dull—a regular and unthinking believing churchgoer for as long as I lived in my parents' home. There I endured the prayers and rituals and kitschy teachings that all seemed Natural and interesting enough at the time (though thanks to the way You guys have explained it, I'm now horrified by such ritual child abuse!). I sang in choirs; read the Bible and other religious mumbo jumbo on my own; attended one or another of Nietzsche's tombs on Sundays, together with biologically related members of my Species. During those years, I must stress again, I was not embarrassed or ashamed of any of this (most cradle Dulls are not), but was still less understanding of the damage it was doing.

Then came the first, if temporary, break with all that: I went off to an American university for four years. There I luxuriated for the first time in the fierce light of Bright ideas and knew briefly that happy Atheist disregard for a great many things that bothered me both before and since.

So far, I was so American-believer typical. But here's where my story starts to get twisted. In my second year I was assigned by sheerest chance to an academic advisor who started me astray. An "agnostic" rather than an "Atheist"—a distinction I now know to be a warning bell, though I didn't know it then!—this retrograde professor saw to it that I take a course that in retrospect appears to be a real potential hassle for our side: a class in formal, symbolic Logic. Some of You might know what I mean here: the system made up of "A" and "not-A" and soundness and validity and proofs and all the rest of that superstitious stuff started by Aristotle and buffed up by the medievals.

And this introduction to Logic, I have no doubt in retrospect, was the beginning of my years of sliding away from the ideas of the Brights and back into the religious wilderness. The funny thing is, I wasn't much interested in religion one way or another during those years. It's just that some contrarian little reflex, apparently kickstarted by that introduction to Logic, kept twitching inside here and there whenever the subject of god versus godlessness came up—and time and again it seemed to say that Atheism wasn't answering some pretty big questions.

Like, one contradiction that waved its hand whenever I thought about Atheism starts as what looks like a simple question: *Where was all this god-believing business coming from in the first place?* Why was it that—with the exceptions of a few Greeks, Spinoza, and a scattering of other Atheist bravehearts whom one could easily name—practically all of human history has been inseparable from belief in *some* deity?

Now, this question of why human beings have been like this—always leaning toward gods, or "theotropic" as some of You like to say (I love Your big words!)—is trickier than it looks for us. In fact, it's trickier I think than any of You guys really understand, which is why it worries me so. For either one produces a satisfying reason for why, say, 99.99999999 percent of humanity has been wrong on that big issue while *You* have been right; or, failing that, one simply comes right out and says that the entire rest of the Species up to oneself was stupid as a bag of rocks till the day before yesterday—a stance that does run the risk, or so I used to think, of looking just a teensy bit arrogant.

Not that that stops some Atheists from risking it! Bertrand Russell, for one, argued pretty much just that in His famous essay, "Why I Am Not a Christian." He declared religion to be based "primarily and mainly upon fear. . . . Fear is the basis of the whole thing—fear of the mysterious, fear of defeat, fear of death." Many other Brights believe the same, I know, including some of You. "Fear, terror and anguish", says major French Atheist

30

Michel Onfray, are "the devices designed to create divinities."

It's not like I'm saying He's wrong, of course! But once again, if You'll just let me explain from the point of view of a former Dull, it seems to *other* people that what we Brights are really saying is, "If *most* of Humanity has turned to religion out of fearfulness, then *I* must be an exceptionally brave and brilliant person to reject that way out." Well, maybe Voltaire and Baron d'Holbach and Bertrand Russell were just such beasts, and maybe some of You are too (*especially* that alpha Atheist Mr. Dawkins—grrrrr!). But speaking as someone who is not, it seemed to me better to give some sort of other explanation for theotropism—I mean, something other than the "I'm a universal genius MUHAHAHAHA and I see things that other mere ordinary mortals don't" kind of explanation (You know, just to avoid this problem of being misconstrued as some unbelievable egomaniac head case or something).

Not that there's anything wrong with putting oneself first, as Nature intended us to! But the egomania thing does hurt us in the Dull trenches, especially with girls; trust me.

Anyway, so if that first Atheist answer to why religion exists at all doesn't satisfy, how about the second one that some of You get behind? According to this *other* explanation, religion is not so much a reaction to bad things as a vain search for good ones; i.e., religion supposedly answers some deep need we have for, say, the "God" of the Old or New Testament. That's what big swinging forebears like Ludwig Feuerbach and Sigmund Freud would have said—that religious beliefs "are illusions, fulfillments of the oldest, strongest, most urgent wishes of mankind", as S.F. once put it. In other words, Loser is really just Daddy with a bigger wallet and more treats.

Now here's why I never went along with that other big line of Atheist argument, which I tell You as only a former Dull could: because nothing about it rings true. Because *that* kind of god, i.e., the Judeo-Christian god, is not remotely the kind of deity that I personally would invent to watch over *me*.

I mean, just think. In Mr. Dawkins' much-quoted description of the Old Testament god in particular, this particular deity was "jealous and proud of it; a petty, unjust, unforgiving control freak; a vindictive, bloodthirsty ethnic cleanser; a misogynistic, homophobic, racist, infanticidal, genocidal, filicidal, pestilential, megalomaniacal, sadomasochistic, capriciously malevolent bully." He's quite a piece of work! Even when I "believed" in "him", I would have grudgingly acknowledged that a list like that has a point.

But don't You see the problem here? The very character of the Judeo-Christian god that has given You such a romp with the adjectives actually turns out to be a pretty big problem for the Atheist side. The point everybody's missing is that this particular god is *hard* to live with—so hard that the Atheist idea of his having been made up just for the supposed "consolation" of it all is just too LOL. Even at his best, he's not the sort of supernatural one can easily cuddle up to. As Graham Greene's fallen whiskey priest puts it in *The Power and the Glory*, making the point that even this god's "love" is pretty scary stuff, "It set fire to a bush in the desert, didn't it, and smashed open graves and set the dead walking in the dark. Oh, a man like me would run a mile to get away if he felt that love around", and a female Human like me too. That's how I felt even back then, the few times when I bothered to stop and think about it.

So You see, this very scariness of this Judeo-Christian god is seriously bad for us—or at least bad for the Atheist claim that he was invented by people to make them feel *better*. Because if the human purpose that keeps calling Loser into existence is some deep search for comfort—if he is just supposed to be some big cosmic Prozac, or a blankie in the sky—I have to tell You this god is seriously not cutting it for me, and not just for me but for a lot of other people as well.

Now on the other hand, a deity who would let me smoke and drink as much as I want, drop five pounds without going a-rex again, string up that judge from juvie court (long story), send my boyfriend packing on the grounds that we Humans aren't "hardwired" to be married for life (so true! but more about that later): now *there's* a god this former believer could have gotten her head around, a god who turns bread into iPod minis and water into Grey Goose vodka—*now* we're getting somewhere! *That's* what I'm talkin' about, if You know what I mean.

But Loser? That pathetic deity who does nothing but talk about *laws, laws, laws,* just about every one of which seems aimed at thwarting what I want most at any given moment—that is, when he's not talking about how I'm supposed to *love, love, love* . . . my *enemies,* of all retarded things? No, *that's* not the sort of ultimate "wish fulfillment" *I* have in mind at all. I hope I'm not getting too personal or giving too much away. But again, I don't think I'm the only one who thinks the wish fulfillment theory is a crock because of items like this.

Another crock is the standard Atheist comeback, i.e., that this Judeo-Christian god promises eternity, and that eternity is what the wish fulfillment is *really* about; after all, who wouldn't want to live forever? But the problem here is that the "eternity offer", at least the one in Judaism and Christianity, has such dorky strings attached. Who'd want it? Ask Yourself, which is more dreamy—a world with no forever in which You can do whatever You want for as long as You live here; or one with a forever that You might spend badly if You blow it here? Hmmm, let's think about that . . . *not*; the answer is pretty obvious if what You want most is fun and games in the here and now. You don't have to be a Natural Scientist to get that one right!

This brings us to one more problem that not one of You guys has addressed no matter how many Dull critics complain about it: all this Atheist talk of wish fulfillment furthermore dumps a big problem of its own down on our side. After all, if metaphysics is something that Humanity just wishes on itself for deep unconscious this-thing-is-bigger-than-the-both-of-us kind of reasons, then where does that fact leave *our* world view, i.e., that of Atheism?

As that professor Alister McGrath—a former one of us who has gone *totally* over to the other side (don't worry, I have a whole Letter about those convert traitor problem cases coming later)—has pointed out, the trouble with wish fulfillment is that it raises the question of what *Atheists* wish for too. In other words, do we Brights want to abolish Loser for reasons of our *own*— because that lets us off the hook to do whatever we please in this world? Is it possible that, as that totally outrageous public enemy Dinesh D'Souza has said, "the reason many atheists are drawn to deny God, and especially the Christian God, is to avoid having to answer in the next life for their lack of moral restraint in this one"?

I hate it when the believers turn our ideas on their heads that way, don't You? But You have to admit, there's a kooky kind of sense in that criticism! *That* kind of potential embarrassment is one more reason to downplay the wish fulfillment "theory", or so this former believer totally advises.

Another problem with learning a bit of Logic was this: just as it helped in locating where a real contradiction might be skulking, so did it illuminate other claims as being *not* contradictory, valid, invalid, and so on. And here again, Atheism lost some points in my book for a while.

Take what some Brights have been making of the fact that there are lots of different religions in the world saying plenty of different things. Many of You have been right out front, going on and on about how all this religious diversity somehow "proves" that not one of those religions can be correct. But of course this is what's called a fallacious inference. The fact that different religions exist doesn't tell you the truth value of any one of them—any more than having twelve answers to a math problem tells You which one is right, say, or having ten pairs of Manolo Blahnik shoes tells You which ones to wear with a cheetah leather skirt.

And just as one can't argue against any *particular* religion by pointing out that another one exists, neither can You really argue with a straight face anyway that god's existence is somehow "disproven" by the complications of a bureaucracy of saints and clergy, or by the many commandments and rituals of Christendom, no matter how twisted and stupid they may be. I know C. S. Lewis isn't anybody's favorite writer here (mine neither!), but I have to admit he got at least this point across. The problem with arguing that Christianity is too complicated to be true, he pointed out, is that the objection doesn't conform with the evidence of our everyday senses. In real life, just about everything of interest is complicated; why should religion be different? And not only that:

Besides being complicated, reality, in my experience is usually odd. It is not neat, not obvious, not what you expect. For instance, when you have grasped that the earth and the other planets all go round the sun, you would naturally expect that all the planets were made to match—all at equal distances from each other, say, or distances that regularly increased, or all the same size, or else getting bigger or smaller as you go farther from the sun.... Reality, in fact, is usually something you could not have guessed. That is one of the reasons I believed Christianity.... It is not the sort of thing anyone would have made up. It has just that queer twist about it that real things have.

Now back to our Movement! I bet that after all this constructive criticism of mine, You're all really starting to wonder how I learned to love Atheism and ignore the contradictions! Aren't You? I hope so! Well, all I can say for now is that it goes to show that there are plenty of things in life that are more important than Logic—and they don't all come from a locked medicine cabinet, either! Not to worry, guys—as Michael says to Pop in *The Godfather*, "We'll get there."

Before that, though, I want to take us on another detour into some other rhetoric that we Atheists need to jettison, and fast, because even the Dulls are beginning to realize how we're handing them plenty of ammunition with it: what the losing side would call the question of "good works".

Adaptively (and helpfully!) Yours,
A. F. Christian

LETTER THREE
The Trouble with Good Works

Dear Friends Messrs. Dawkins, Dennett, Harris, Hitchens, Onfray, Stenger, and Others (again),

As I explained in my first Letter, I really do believe that one of the most important contributions I can make as a newly converted Atheist is to let You know what is and isn't working for our side when it comes to winning the so-called hearts and minds of the rest of our Species. In some areas, as I observed about sex (!), it's *definitely* better for us Brights just to change the subject and not to compete with the believers at all.

It's like they keep telling me in this place, some things are just bigger than You are, and there's no point in even trying to pretend You're in control. The same goes for us Atheists too! Sometimes You just have to cut Your losses and hit "control-alt-delete".

One big case in point is "good works", or the question of who is more likely to be on good behavior with the lesser members of the Species—us or the believers. And here, as a matter of general strategy, I cannot stress enough something that some of You are just refusing to get: *we Atheists are much better off emphasizing what the other side has done wrong rather than emphasizing anything we Brights have done right.*

After all, two thousand years of Christianity have given us plenty of ammunition to use against our adversaries without our having to fight pathetic battles in the field. I mean, appreciate our resources here! Here's just *some* of what we can throw in the Catholics' faces alone: any number of popes, a way higher number of bishops, at least some of the faculty and administration at both Georgetown and Notre Dame, and—thanks to the latest round of priest-boy sex scandals—even whole orders and seminaries (You know the ones I mean) striving day and night to undermine the "Church"! There are all *kinds* of corrupt clergy who are doing more to give Loser a bad name, just by the atrocity of their examples, than anything we Atheists could *possibly* dream up or execute ourselves. Not to mention all those influential lay Web sites and public figures who dish out awesome piles of cafeteria Catholicism. You know—the ones whose Catholicism amounts to cherry picking what they like about Loser's books and leaving out all the parts they don't! Seriously, how could we possibly confuse matters among the papists any more than they already have themselves?

And if the Catholic Church has been the cake, some of the Protestants have been perfect frosting. All those Mainline clergy delivering Christianity Lite—have a little appreciation for how much preachers like these help us out! Just think how much harder it was for our side back in the beginning, when the Dulls' stupid books were fresher in their cerebral cortexes and the Christians were actually being all pious and suffering in the Colosseum and planting themselves more firmly on the "moral high ground"! How about another little "Thank you!" to those renegades like Warren Jeffs who pop up alongside their twenty wives and fifty kids as regular as desert clockwork, leaving us Atheists to hoot and holler profitably about our biggest asset, "religious hypocrisy". Talk about getting manna from somewhere!

Add to those any number of historical fiascos, whether real or exaggerated, and You'll see that we Atheists can undermine *lots* of believers, simply by emphasizing how badly *a few* of them have behaved—and again, we don't need to get too far off the historical reservation to do it.

But we Brights do *not* need to, and in fact should not ever, take the unnecessary further step of crediting our own side with *good* behavior. In fact, if I could have offered our new Movement one single bit of advice on this, it would have been: *Don't even go there.*

But would any of You have listened? *Ahem?* Unfortunately, just about nobody has grasped the point.

41

Here is Mr. Daniel Dennett, for example, waaaaaay out on the very limb I'm warning about: "There is *no reason at all* why a disbelief in the immateriality or immortality of the soul should make a person less caring, less moral, less committed to the well-being of everybody on Earth than somebody who believes in 'the spirit'" (italics are His). And Mr. Sam Harris: "The fact that faith has motivated many people to do good things does not suggest that faith is itself a necessary (or even a good) motivation for goodness." Everybody, and not just You guys but others in the history of our Movement, seems to agree about this: the believers must not be allowed to claim that religion at its best makes people behave well—or even better than they would behave without it.

Now if You all just think for a minute, You'll know as well as I do why this is so damaging for us: because *the actual evidence for claiming that Atheism will do as much good in the world as Christianity and other religions is embarrassingly against us.*

I'm not even talking here about the tired charges made by the other side about what happens when Atheists actually *run* the world—mass murder, genocide, concentration camps, and the rest of the twentieth-century record. Of course plenty of people *do* want to rub our noses in history, the twerps. Papal point man Michael Novak appears to have been running especially annoying defense lately. I mean, that crack of his about how

Mr. Sam Harris tries to "explain away the horrors of the self-declared atheist regimes in modern history: Fascist in Italy, Nazi in Germany, and Communist in the Soviet Union": ouch! That one had to hurt, even if it was totally off the wall in any historic sense. As if any one of those governments could top the Inquisition in a body count! Right?

Equally annoying are the people who argue that the record doesn't support Your claim that Nazis and Communists and whatnot were *really* somehow religious underneath—You know, as if Paula Abdul on *American Idol* was *secretly* a fat bald male teetotaler whose skin is Naturally almost as tight as Hillary Clinton's. If You ask me, that mathematician and nonbeliever David Berlinski gives the "secretly religious" theory a real smack in his treacherous recent attack on us, *The Devil's Delusion*:

What Hitler did *not* believe and what Stalin did *not* believe and what Mao did *not* believe and what the SS did *not* believe and what the Gestapo did *not* believe and what the NKVD did *not* believe and what the commissars, functionaries, swaggering executioners, Nazi doctors, Communist Party theoreticians, intellectuals, Brown Shirts, Black Shirts, gauleiters, and a thousand party hacks did *not* believe was that God was watching what they were doing.

All this in one sentence too! What a pain Berlinski is. He might as well be working under the table for Loser. I wouldn't be surprised. (Idea: The next time You guys want to burn something, let's start with his book!)

Now, I know how those trumped-up accusations about Atheist murder and genocide and whatever annoy us Brights, so I'm not going to dwell on this any further. I'm worried instead about something related that *hasn't* gotten the same attention as the little "excesses" of our recent history, but could be just as harmful to our side if the Dulls started looking at it. It's the fact that the religious people in the West, generally speaking, take better care of the sick and weak than do Secularists and Atheists, *and they know it.*

Hospitals, soup kitchens, social services, charitable networks, missions, prison ministries, orphanages, clinics, and all those other institutions embodying the distasteful fixation of the believers on the weak—now how can we Atheists possibly compete with all that? The Catholics: 615 hospitals, 1,600 local agencies under Catholic Charities, over 7,500 schools and 221 colleges and universities; lay organizations, such as the Knights of Columbus, Black and Indian Missions, Society of St. Vincent de Paul, and several hundred more engaged in charitable activity—all just in America. And that's not to say the papists are the only ones who have it going on—so do the Jews, the Muslims, and the Protestants.

Look at the evangelicals with their nonstop pathetic outreaches of all kinds and their foreign missions too—into which they shovel some $2.5 billion a year.

Then there are the Mormons, and I would most *definitely* not want us Atheists messing with the Church of Jesus Christ of Latter-day Saints in any kind of goody-off contest. What's the number one American city for charitable giving? Salt Lake City. Where are four of the ten American counties where charitable giving is highest? Right next to Salt Lake City. Oh, but You say, that's all for the Church of Latter-day Saints, hence suspect. Yet according to the Bureau of Labor Statistics, the state where volunteering, i.e., coaching, collecting food, etc., is highest is also Utah.

One of the *worst* things that's happened lately for all those claims of Yours that believers and nonbelievers are morally equivalent in their behavior toward others in the Species is the publishing of another horrible recent book. This one's by econo-brain Arthur C. Brooks and is called *Who Really Cares: America's Charity Divide; Who Gives, Who Doesn't, and Why It Matters*. Geeking over what he calls "the fruit of years of analysis on the best national and international datasets available on charity, lots of computational horsepower, and the past work of dozens of scholars who have looked at various bits and pieces of the charity puzzle", numbers-nerd Brooks shows beyond a doubt one fact that our side should *not* want out: that American believers are more "generous" in every sense than the enlightened likes of us.

Brooks says that religious people give more to charity than nonreligious people—in fact, much more: "An enormous charity gap", he reports, "remains between religious and secular people."

> To see this, imagine two women who are both forty-five years old, white, married, have an annual household income of $50,000, and attended about a year of college. The only difference between them is that one goes to church every week, but the other never does. The churchgoing woman will be 21 percentage points more likely to make a charitable gift of money during the year than the nonchurchgoer, and she will also be 26 points more likely to volunteer. Furthermore, she will tend to give $1,383 more per year to charity, and to volunteer on 6.4 more occasions.

Brooks goes on to test the charity gap up, down, and sideways. The results are always the same:

> People who pray every day (whether or not they go to church) are 30 percentage points more likely to give money to charity than people who never pray (83 to 53 percent). And people saying they

devote a "great deal of effort" to their spiritual lives are 42 points more likely to give than those devoting "no effort" (88 to 46 percent). Even a belief in *beliefs themselves* is associated with charity. People who say that "beliefs don't matter as long as you're a good person" are dramatically less likely to give charitably (69 to 86 percent) and to volunteer (32 to 51 percent) than people who think that beliefs *do* matter.

In fact, it's not even all dollars and cents. Brooks also reports that religious people volunteer more than Seculars—and even give more Species blood!

Now leaving that nasty little bit of empiricism aside, there's an even bigger problem for us in this talk of good works. It's that the Dulls do not only do this charitable stuff because their backward books tell them to; they also think that helping the weak is a good thing to do *just in and of itself.* And as long as they persist in believing such an unnatural thing, it will be hard for us Atheists to bring them in by promising that the unbelievers do better at this game. They're stupid, yes—but not *that* stupid.

As a Dull child, for example, I personally knew a Catholic priest who left a comfortable suburban parish to start up a mission—in a part of the country of Togo so awful that it makes Calcutta look like something out of *How to Marry a Millionaire.* Just the pictures of his well-digging, barefooted, pretty needy-looking African clients probably kept me in the believers' ranks longer than anything else. I don't know even know why, mind You! After all, I was not closely genetically related to these people, so the continuance of their DNA was neither here nor there for me. But something about that priest's risky involvement with them got under my skin, and it also seemed somehow to reflect well on the religion in whose name he did these things.

That's the psychological effect of this kind of selfless behavior by others on Your average believer. It's like an addiction with them. I appreciate that Mr. Hitchens at least tried to address this problem with his hardy-har-har attempted takedown of Mother Teresa. But it failed totally. Even most of our allies in the Secular media (and they are legion, as You know!) were embarrassed by it. What's the point of arguing that You shouldn't do good things with bad money, which seems to be Mr. Hitchens' only coherent point? What are You *supposed* to do with bad money—bad things only? Do You know how lame this kind of "Pick me! Pick me!" variation of Atheist journalism looks to everyone else?

For another example, consider how things look if we compare, say, western Europe (which thankfully is largely post-Christian now) with the U.S. (still occupied outside the major cities by Dulls). Do You remember what happened in Secular France in the summer of 2003? How about some 14,800 "excess deaths" (I love that word, "excess"), mostly among the old, mostly in that citadel of civilization, gay Paree? That's just an official French estimate, by the way; others were higher. Some of those old bodies were never even claimed, just laid out in those plain, thin wood rectangular boxes outside Paris like Pottery Barn Teen was having the biggest outdoor mattress and box spring sale ever, or something.

Now, everyone official says he knows the reasons why this happened—because of heat topping 100 degrees during a month when most of the city, including much of the nursing home staff, went on vacation. Well, there's Secular Europe for You: Granmamma's in a "home" getting heatstroke, and her family, or what remains of it, is too busy with Eurail and Ryanair and vacation oohla-la to care. And so Nature got to dispose of a whole lot of unfit people at one swoop. Now, I'm not saying that's a bad thing, any more than any other real Darwinist would. But my point is, does anyone really believe this would have happened if France were still a Christian country?

Not that plenty of atrocities didn't happen when France *was* Christian! But the point is, would this *particular* atrocity, i.e., the totally freaky abandonment of the old and sick and weak in one of the most modern cities on earth in the name of *leisure*, have happened if

Christianity still colored the way people behave in Europe? Was it thinkable in a world where what the religious call "the family" still had force behind it? For that matter, does anyone think it would have happened if all those geezers had been *Muslims* rather than post-Christian Europeans?

No, no, and no, and all for the same reason: because organized religion would have intervened. The American Christian response after Hurricane Katrina, to take one counterexample right in our faces, was as fast as the American government's was lame.

But then again, why should the believers' edge in caring for the unfit surprise us Atheists? After all, it's not as if hospitals and soup kitchens abound in our inner cities in Darwin's name. There's not exactly a Bright network within the prisons bringing aid and comfort to the people inside. And it's not like the sociologically unfit show up at the American Atheist headquarters or the Natural History Museum, say, when it's thirty degrees below outside and they want a blanket and a bowl of free slop. Oh, and how about the many Atheist families who have adopted six or eight or ten children, including those with handicaps? Right! I don't know any either.

And that's just my point: not only should our side refuse to compete on fronts like these when there's no evidence to our credit anyways; we should also be clear among ourselves that *we Atheists don't want the kind of world in which Nature's rejects, the sick and the old and the frail of any sort, flourish anyway.*

That's what upsets me so much about Your collective insistence that Atheism can pick up the moral slack of religion in the matter of good works. It's so hypocritical! Do we *really* want a society, say, abounding in family-minded people who take in other people's unfit offspring? Next thing You know, after *that*, people might get the idea of protecting, say, crippled infants, or people in comas, or Alzheimer's or Parkinson's patients, or other unfortunate parasites on our Species. And how Natural is any of that? Answer: *Not!*

No, competing against the believers on grounds of good behavior will do our side no good at all. I urge You with all my DNA to stay away from that game. The reason why we'll lose it every time is simple: because *their* highest authority, Loser, tells them to care for the sick and weak, whereas ours, Nature, tells us the opposite.

The trick to end-running it is clear enough: just keep focused at all times on the evils committed in religion's name. Never mind how long ago they were! Try not to let the Dulls point out that You are comparing religious apples (i.e., what institutionalized religion did in Europe *six hundred* years ago) with Atheist oranges (i.e., what institutionalized Atheism did in Europe *sixty* years ago). Mercifully, as it were, many of them are just ignorant enough of history not to call our bluffs on rhetorical saves like that.

But never, never, never pretend that we have a code that would in any way render us as attentive to Nature's castoffs as the Dulls are, because we don't—and not only do we not have one, but in principle we *do not want one*. And next, before introducing You to my former boyfriend Lobo (!), which is where my own conversion story really begins, I want to get going on a couple of other kinds of Bright chatter that need to be dialed down in the future for our Movement's sake. Remember, I'm only here to help!

Yours empirically 4-ever,
A. F. Christian

LETTER FOUR
The Trouble with Dull Art

Dear All You Major-League Atheist Guys,

First up today, a little technical note. Apparently, some people who call themselves Your "friends" have been trying to e-mail me in here lately. I know because the Director just came by to tell me that all their mail went straight to the spam file. He said they were in violation of the following rules: (1) No letters that are WRITTEN ENTIRELY IN CAPS get through the filters here; (2) neither do any using the F-word; and (3) neither do any with misspellings (that one was at my own request—I think those kinds of mistakes make us Atheists look unscientific!).

Anyway, the Director said rules (2) and (3) alone knocked out just about everything that was incoming to me from those so-called friends. Sorry about that, guys, but I thought You should know. I felt kind of bad for You after he told me. I sure hope everybody gets a better class of correspondent! You all deserve it, that's for sure! That's part of why I'm writing so much, I hope You know.

Now back to today's set of advice about our godless Movement and what's best for it: this Letter is about another set of issues that blocked my own conversion to Atheism for some time, though I'm almost embarrassed to admit it now. But since they're issues that are keeping many another believer in Loser's corner and out of our godless reach, I really need to explain to You how vulnerable they make us Atheists. These are what might loosely be called the problems of Dull achievement.

By "achievement" I don't mean this time the soup kitchens and hospitals and schools and missions and all that sort of feel-good charitable slop that I talked about in the last Letter. I mean instead that higher record on which the believers perpetually pride themselves—in architecture, music, sculpture, painting, literature, philosophy, and the aesthetic life. I'm talking about their infuriating claim that religion is inseparable from— even *responsible* for—artistic achievement of the very first order.

Now, before anybody chucks a spaz and starts learning spell-check to try and get around the e-mail filters in here, let me state the obvious right up front: no, this is *not* the kind of question that settles the biggest issue one way or another. Nothing about the architecture and art and poetry and music and all that fluffy stuff definitively establishes the *existence* of Loser.

But that's precisely what makes this aesthetic claim of the Dulls so bad for us, don't You see? They think in the most annoying superior way imaginable that this *suggestive* evidence is powerful enough. They argue that the best of religiously inspired art is of such transcendent quality that it can be explained *only* as a window of some kind onto a reality higher, or more perfect, or more lasting than this one.

Further, the Dulls contend in the most annoying offhand way that this best of religious art is unmatched by aesthetic efforts of *any* other kind (let alone the belligerently Secular stuff of, say, Communist "drama" or sculpture or architecture). In other words, they smugly let their religious art *speak for itself*—a posture that has brought many an unwitting aesthete dangerously close to a Dull point of view and even pushed some over the edge into religious belief.

Okay, let's admit that they have a thing or two in their corner—St. Mark's Basilica in Venice, Notre Dame in Paris, St. Peter's Basilica in Rome, the Hohe Domkirche St. Peter und Maria in Cologne, Santa Maria del Fiore in Florence, the Duomo of Milan, St. Paul's Cathedral in London, and so braggedy-brag on. And that's just starters for Dull architecture, as You know. Then there are the like-minded raisings of all kinds of magnificent temples and mosques and stupas and such by other kinds of believers, also all over the world and also all throughout history. The obvious fact that we Atheists have yet to wrap our heads around is that most of the world's greatest buildings, and I mean "greatest" aesthetically, not literally, have been dedicated in one way or another to Loser, by whatever name he's called in any given spot.

Don't get me wrong, guys—I'm not saying Frank Gehry and Le Corbusier and downtown Pyongyang aren't all that! But still.

This aesthetic ammunition of the Dulls only gets worse the more You look at it. Add to the architecture just *some* of the written record—the so-called scriptures (and even You admit there are some pretty good one-liners in there!), the *City of God*, the *Divine Comedy*, the *Praise of Folly*, the *Summa Theologica*, blahbidy blah blah; or, say, an impressive if deluded pack of rabbis, scholars, priests, nuns, theologians, mystics, poets, soldiers, yadda, yadda—all testifying through the ages in Loser's name. Plus, and there's no point even arguing with this one, the believers can also claim all the best music for human voices ever written, *and* every painting and sculpture of any real worth whatsoever from the fall of Rome onward.

I'm trying to keep this short, guys! These kinds of lists could fill a library (come to think of it, these kinds of lists are what libraries are made of). Yet annoying though it is to have to acknowledge the extent of such achievement in Loser's name, we Atheists do have to grant that the believers aren't making that particular record up.

Now, this aesthetic legacy of religion isn't anything that You all have paid much attention to, I realize. For reasons I'm not sure of (but maybe someone will explain someday), the facts of beauty and sublimity don't seem to be issues to which Atheists are sensitive—period.

I'm not even sure why I still feel them myself, so long after my own turn to Atheism. It's true that when my ex-boyfriend, Lobo, got stoned, there was nothing he liked better than opening all his dad's coffee-table books on Renaissance art and eyeballing the paintings and sculptures. And it's true that this was one of the few things Lobo did that I enjoyed doing with him when I wasn't stoned myself. That was before his dad kicked him out and we moved to Portland, You know. I'm not saying Lobo was *all* bad, by the way. Just mostly. That's what happens when You pick up Your boyfriend in rehab, I guess!

More about all that later. As I was saying, and regardless of how much we'd like to avoid it, the question for us Atheists about this religious art is really very simple: Do the Dulls have a point about this aesthetic record, or do they not? Were these works, and others that are considered to be among Humanity's masterpieces, even *thinkable* apart from religion itself? In other words, is there a *necessary* (as opposed to accidental) connection between the exaltedness of the art, and that of the religion from which it claims inspiration and derivation?

Again with all due respect, it doesn't help with this aesthetic problem to have Mr. Hitchens diss it by saying that "we [Atheists] have music and art and literature, and find that the serious ethical dilemmas are better handled by Shakespeare and Tolstoy and Schiller and Dostoevsky and George Eliot than in the mythical morality tales of the holy books." Never mind the first problem here, i.e., how many of those names on his greatest-hits list were Dulls themselves. And never mind, or try to anyway, the question of what explicitly Atheist music and art and literature actually *look* like—I mean, it's not as if Futurism and Constructivism and Abstract Expressionism and Performance Art never existed! BTW, we'd be *much* better off if they hadn't. (New idea: After we get done burning David Berlinski's book against You, can we burn some of that Atheist art too? It sure might help us on the convert front!)

The critical point here is this: we Atheists must not let ourselves get trapped into this kind of aesthetic bean counting as Mr. Hitchens does here, because there's no possible world in which we win it. *All* the Dulls, even the least schooled among them, think that this record of art and music and literature devoted to religion across the centuries is some kind of big propaganda plus for them. And they're not the only ones who make that connection, either. "Without having seen the Sistine Chapel one can form no appreciable idea of what one man is capable of achieving"—these traitorous words are from that über-Humanist, Johann Wolfgang von Goethe. Ouch! That one hurts!

In sum, the believers stubbornly insist that the most towering minds in history have willingly harnessed themselves to the cause of religion, and that the record of their achievements speaks for itself. I know it's all completely unscientific! But that doesn't stop the Loser lovers from scoring points with it.

For example, in his very annoying book analyzing post-Christian Europe, *The Cube and the Cathedral*, professional papist George Weigel—who like Michael Novak is one of the sharper of the Dulls—boils down the question of religious art versus Secular art to two symbols: Notre Dame Cathedral in Paris versus that statement of Modernism incarnate, La Grande Arche de la Défense.

Weigel pits these two architectural icons against one another in a contest as follows:

Which culture, I wondered, would better protect human rights? Which culture would more firmly

59

secure the moral foundations of democracy? The culture that built this stunning, rational, angular, geometrically precise but essentially featureless cube? Or the culture that produced the vaulting and bosses, the gargoyles and flying buttresses, the nooks and crannies, the asymmetries and holy "unsameness" of Notre Dame and the other great Gothic cathedrals of Europe?

You see that this inquiry only *appears* to be some thumb-sucker about one old building versus another. It is actually far worse for us Atheists than most other academic-sounding debates. It dangerously connects that judgment about beauty to the question of exactly *what* ideas are embodied in things like the Great Arch. It asks which kind of civilization really puts man and woman at the center and takes best care of them. Again, I'm not taking sides on this, just pointing out for our own protection that the Dulls are definitely on to something in the factual record here.

Not that this makes their harping on it any less frustrating, of course! In connecting his dots between the history of Christianity and European achievement, Weigel actually has the nerve to list for four and a half pages the names of what he calls "larger-than-life personalities . . . all motivated in their life's work by Christian conviction"—Adalbert, Konrad Adenauer, Albert the Great, Ambrose of Milan, Fra Angelico, Anskar, Thomas Aquinas, Athanasius, Augustine of Canterbury, Augustine of Hippo; those are just the A's, and the list goes on through Huldrych Zwingli, if any of You remember who he is (major-league Swiss Reformation guy, if that helps).

Now, You might dismiss Weigel with his witchy old list as just another flack of the mackerel-snappers. He is after all the biographer of that *total* tool and mercifully (as it were) deceased major enemy of ours, John Paul II. But the problem is, he's obviously on to something. A little learning, it's said, is a dangerous thing, and never is it as true as with our Christian adversaries. If only they could not read, or were wholly in ignorance of history—if only they had simply evolved without eyes or ears!—then they wouldn't be so susceptible to believing that there's a connection between aesthetics and eternity in the first place. It doesn't help that most people, Dull *or* Bright, agree that the greatest art in history has been created in the name of Loser—or in the case of the Greeks and Romans, the losers plural, I guess.

And against this Dull artistic excellence, what exactly do we Atheists bring to the table? The Brooklyn Museum of Art? Elton John? Your books? Freak dancing? Rammstein? And note that once again I'm not even *going* to the question of what kind of aesthetics were generated by the specific subgenre of Communist

Atheism proper, about which the less said (as You all seem to understand!) the better. Even Lobo, who was not exactly Mensa bait, couldn't even *walk* by the Whitney Museum without elbowing me and clapping his hands to his face and moaning loudly, "My eyes—they burn! They *buuuuurn*!" while other people stopped to stare at him. I have to admit, I thought it was kind of funny at the time. Even though by then I'd more or less stopped going to church myself and caring one way or the other about art—or much of anything else. That's how hard the art habit dies.

In sum, given the weight of the empirical evidence, I think our most prudent course as Atheists is to stay as far from the questions of aesthetics as possible. I say this even knowing that some potential Brights will be turned themselves by it, lost to us forever in just this impulsively emotional way—undone, say, by Palestrina or the Spanish Baroque; by that tension five hundred years later in the marble index finger of the virgin, playing with the infant's toes in da Settignano's *Foulc Madonna*; or maybe by one of Tiepolo's fat schmaltzy cherubs or a chance reading of a psalm; even by the strains of evensong, floating out of one of Nietzsche's tombs late on a winter's day. How annoyingly little it takes to lose a soul! (*Sorreeeee* again.)

As You can tell, despite my own personal evolution, I'm still all too aware of the way that religious

aesthetics can stab us Brights in the back. In my ignorance as a believer, I once would have argued that there
was more beauty in any single room of the Accademia
in Venice, Santa Croce in Florence, and any square yard
of the Uffizi than in the Whitney and MoMA and the
Pompidou put together.

And like the believer I once was, I'd also have con-
nected that judgment about beauty to another, more
metaphysical one. I would have told You that whatever
was inspiring these disparate people from across time
and languages and cultures to raise such unearthly,
inhumanly gorgeous images and words and sounds—
well, I'd have said the odds were that this religious art
was being inspired by something rather than nothing.
That's Dull psychology for You. That's how the dupes
think.

In sum, for us Atheists, competing against the believers on the field of aesthetics—like competing over good
works or sexual liberation or Logic—is another game
we need to run like crazy from. Personally I'm over it
now, the same way people everywhere break other powerful habits: cold turkey, and no longer going near the
stuff. In short, I just say *nein*!* And so, I advise, should
we all.

I know You're probably getting impatient by now,
and I'm *almost* there as promised on filling You in about
what parts of the new Atheism *did* turn this former

Christian around! First, though, we Brights all need to put our heads together about one more major problem that's keeping our numbers down out there. I'm talking about the many high-profile traitors who have left us for Loser recently—and what to do about those pathetic nastorious wormbags.

TTYL, stay tuned, guys!
XXO, A. F. Christian

*P.S. I just love German, don't You? Talk about the language of Atheism! I'm studying it on Rosetta Stone now, how cool is that? The Director's assistants gave me a set. They said I could practice all I like, as long as I slide the CDs back through the slot before lights out. *Jawohl, mein Kommandant!*

LETTER FIVE
Those Obnoxious Christian Convert Traitors—and What to Do about Them

Dear Major Atheist Author BFFs,

I just *love* calling You that! Is it okay with You if I do? The Director said it was fine with him, because he knows that the *B* means "Best" and the *F*'s mean "Friends Forever". So before going into one more Letter that I hope will help this new Atheism of ours get off the ground, let this convert to godlessness tell You just how *much* You're all my BFFs, and why it's so important that You are.

One, I hope everybody gets that just because I use "BFF" in the plural doesn't mean I'm taking any *one* of You for my BFF in particular. This is important! I don't want, say, Mr. Christopher Hitchens to feel excluded because He thinks I'm talking about, say, Mr. Daniel Dennett as my *particular* BFF.

This is true even though Mr. Hitchens might otherwise have reason to worry about my confidence in Him, since anyone who has converted or deconverted as many times as He has on other big subjects—Marxism, abortion, imperialism, smoking—is obviously the *most* likely of any of us Atheists to jump ship for Loser someday. I'd even bet my tokens for the convenience store in here on that. But that doesn't mean Mr. Hitchens can't be my BFF too in His own way, just like that less volatile Atheist Mr. Daniel Dennett is—because this former Christian is loyal to *all* You big Brights like that.

Mr. Victor J. Stenger, same. He's my BFF too, even if His book didn't get as much attention as some of the other new Atheist ones did. It's not His fault, You know. He's just not as good at *ad hominem* argument as some of You other leading Brights. Or maybe it's because He doesn't go postal on the Jews and their god with the gusto that certain other Atheists do? (You know who You are, guys!) Whatever, even if He isn't a typical Bright for the aforementioned reasons, Mr. Stenger can be my BFF too!

Similarly, I don't want, say, Mr. Sam Harris to think I prefer Mr. Michel Onfray on intellectual grounds—even if Mr. Onfray *does* have that big-unintelligible-words French thing going on, and even if Mr. Harris' last book *was* so small that they could slip it right under the door in this place and not even have to use the pass-through thing (not that there's anything wrong with a short book!). And flipping it around, I also would not want Mr. Onfray to think I prefer Mr. Harris, even though Mr. Harris at least writes in full sentences (if not always in full books!). And not. In cryptic. Esoteric to say the least. Fragments of knowing. Allusions translated from the French. Like Mr. Onfray does. That do not always. Make sense.

But again, that doesn't mean that Mr. Harris and Mr. Onfray and I can't all be BFFs too, just like I am seriously down with that *total* alpha Atheist, Richard Dawkins (*grrrr!*). "I shall not go out of my way to offend, but nor shall I don kid gloves to handle religion any more gently than I would handle anything else": I'm telling You, just *thinking* about that quote from *The God Delusion* sets my evolved inner wiring to "vibrate" like nothing else! So needless to say, Mr. Dawkins is my BFF, maybe even what You might call my über-BFF too.

I hope You guys followed all that! Because this talk about how we Atheists are all Best Friends Forever is totally on point with the urgent subject of today's Letter, namely, our pathetic creeptastic sellout scumbag Dull ENEMIES. And most especially, our *Todfeinde.**

Take a look for starters at the following quote:

Now atheists come in different sorts. There is the rather gracious type who doesn't personally believe in "God", but is very happy if other people find the idea meaningful. And then there is the rather aggressive, intolerant sort, who regards people who believe in "God" as fools, knaves and liars, and wants to rid the world of them. I have to tell you that I was in that second category.

As some of You might recognize, this is one of many cheap shots lobbed against Atheism by the intensely irritating religious convert Alister McGrath—formerly a Scientist doing something called molecular biophysics, later a professor of something called historical theology at Oxford, among other posts; former president of the Oxford Centre for Christian Apologetics; and author of any number of books, including *The Dawkins Delusion?* and *The Twilight of Atheism* and many more—all of which diss everything we Atheists believe in from the point of view of a quote unquote Scientist who *used* to be an Atheist himself, and who isn't one anymore because of the alleged "evidence" against us.

In other words, a *total* traitor enemy combatant Loserlover guy.

And is McGrath the end of this traitor problem for us? As Stuart Larkin, a *Mad TV* character who was my hero for a while after I stopped going to church and before I met You guys, used to say, *Nooooooooooo* ...

which brings me to today's *major* point about our struggle against the Dulls.

Frankly, it makes us Atheists look like *losers*, note the small *l* there, that the believers have so many more converts than we do—and by "converts" I don't mean the cradle types whose noses have been stuck to the altar stone from day one. I mean the ones who have known both the Bright and Dull sides of the argument inside and out—and who went on to betray *ours*.

These guys (and girls! Yes, Loser's side, unlike ours, has plenty of girls!) get under my skin like no one else. It's bad enough that there are so many Dull converts, both now and for the past couple of millennia. It's bad enough that so many have been ranked among the chief brainos of their time. But what *really* jerks my chain is something even worse.

It's that religious conversion, with the notable exception of Your humble servant here, is almost always a one-way street—and not only now, but going back to, say, Paul. Many a formerly firm Atheist has become a Dull. But nowhere *near* as many firm Dulls, I mean *real* religious believers, have become Atheists. That's what burns me up (as it were!) about all those converts. It's like they always get to be the cool "after" car on *Pimp My Ride*—and we Atheists are almost always stuck being the dorky who'd-really-want-to-drive-this "before" one.

I don't mean that we Brights haven't gotten good at picking off many an agnostic or so-what kind of Human. Of course we score big time with the young guys who aren't responsible for anything and don't really care about anything besides spending most of their time in the basement playing video games, watching porn, and texting girls unsuccessfully and firing off the occasional crazy blog or e-mail in between making runs to the fridge for booze and Red Bull and leftover pizza. Those folks are easy enough pickings for us, as You know. And don't get me wrong—I'm not knocking them! It's not like our Atheist ranks don't depend on the loyalty of guys like that!

But getting *serious* people over to our side, once Loser's Word is *really* planted inside them? Forget about it! Just look at some of the most annoying traitor convert cases from the twentieth century alone. In Britain and just for starters, we have Evelyn Waugh, C.S. Lewis, Malcolm Muggeridge, Graham Greene, Edith Sitwell, Siegfried Sassoon, Hilaire Belloc, G.K. Chesterton, Dorothy Sayers, and T.S. Eliot.

In fact, there are so *many* Brit converts from that era that they're the subject of an entire book called *Literary Converts: Spiritual Inspiration in an Age of Unbelief*. It was written by—what else?—one Joseph Pearce, a Dull convert who claimed he was himself turned by another convert, or should I say in this case überconvert: G. K. Chesterton.

That's one good example of how the religious insanity gets transmitted. For a few more examples of crackpot converts, how about Mortimer Adler, Clare Boothe Luce, Kit Carson, Frederick Copleston, Dorothy Day, Elizabeth Fox-Genovese, Antonia Fraser, Peter Geach, René Girard, Alec Guinness, Frederick Hart, Gerard Manley Hopkins, E. Howard Hunt, Russell Kirk? And that's just cherry picking through A–K on Wikipedia for the names I think You all would recognize; there are plenty more out there that You might not know.

Let's focus for a minute on my own personal nominee for worst-case traitor Dull of all time. That would be G. E. M.—the *E* is for "Elizabeth", which is a female name, if You see where I'm going with this—Anscombe.

Have You ever heard the phrase "having it all"? Apparently, nobody told her she couldn't. She was not only a woman, but a mother; not only a mother, but a mother of seven; not only a mother of seven, but married; not only a mother of seven and married, but happily married (to another genius, philosopher and logician Peter Geach); not all that but also a professor; not only all that plus a professor, but also at Cambridge; not only all *that*, but typically described as the most significant female philosopher of the twentieth century—and a confidante of Ludwig Wittgenstein, whose *Philosophical*

Investigations are still read in her translation—and not to put too fine a point on it, she was *another* backstabbing Christian traitor convert, C-O-N-V-E-R-T, from early on.

And she never, ever shut up about Loser, either. Not even when times were bad for the "Church", like in the 1960s, and she defended all the most unpopular Dull teachings. Not even when times were good, and she won acclaim for all kinds of things, including some nonreligious monograph called *Intention*, which most eggheads call one of the most important works of analytic philosophy of its time. She didn't even stop talking about Loser when she kicked the bucket! Even her *obituary* read: "She was attended on her deathbed by four of her seven children, all of whom are practicing Catholics." Talk about rubbing it in!

Do You guys have any idea how much this Anscombe thing alone hurts us? My bad! I forgot: Atheists don't seem to know many women. But let's pretend You did, and let's say You were playing our favorite Bright "brain game" with one of them—You know, the one that goes, "Come join us Atheists, my little chickadee, because that's where all the Scientists and brainiacs are!" Well, what do You do if someone up and asks something like, Well, what about Elizabeth Anscombe? Wouldn't even some of You be just a *little* set back? I mean, I've read Your books and I've read hers too, and it's not like that comparison exactly proves that all the I.Q. points are in the Bright corner!

Okay, forget about G. E. M. Anscombe! I admit, I'm a little obsessed there. Even sketchy ex-boyfriend Lobo could see that. That's part of why he gave me Your books, You know; more on that episode in a later Letter. For now, let's focus instead on the many other Humans who have made the same trip to Loser's side like Anscombe did, and who also haven't come back. I mean even after Darwin! After Ayn Rand! Even after Eddie Vedder went atheo too!

I'm not making fun of our Bright celebrities, of course. I just wish some of You wouldn't make quite so much of them. It makes me nervous, because a lot of the names we Atheists brag about just don't measure up to the ones the Dulls can claim—like, way. Sometimes it feels like the believers are all getting to play *Halo 3*, while we Atheists are still stuck on *Mario Speedwagon*.

And the convert cases just keep coming. In Washington, D.C., alone during the past few years—yes, the past few years, exactly the time when this new Atheism of ours has been rolled out for discussion everywhere—any number of high-profile journalists and politicians have jumped ship for Loser and taken the flak for it. And in more strategic bad news, we Brights lost an absolutely critical ally when Bernard

Nathanson—formerly one of America's chief abortion- ists and an actual founder of the fantabulous group NARAL, *go, team!*—went over to Loser's side. He said it was all because of the *sonogram machine*; can You believe such a pathetic reason as that?

Now why can't we Atheists snag somebody high pro- file like that? Maybe we should start a TV show called *America's Top Atheists*, where the winners get to burn books by enemy religious converts! (How about Vox Day's *The Irrational Atheist: Dissecting the Unholy Trinity of Dawkins, Harris, and Hitchens*, for starters!) Do You think that might help?

And Bernard Nathanson is just the beginning of our worst enemies of all, i.e., those converts who also know Science. That Francis Collins of the Human Genome Project is *especially* in need of a takedown, in the opin- ion of this Bright. His argument that sequencing the human genome was what turned him Christian has done more damage to Atheism than just about anything else the Dulls have thrown at us lately. By the way, I notice that apart from one teeny-tiny mention of Collins in Mr. Dawkins' book, the rest of You have avoided talk- ing about those Scientists who are also religious believ- ers. It's just a little thing, of course. But given the propaganda damage they've done, You might want to fix that in forthcoming editions so You're not accused of ignoring something important!

But enough of this Debbie Downer stuff for now. Let's look at the Bright side, as it were, that is, what we can do about these traitor cases!

Fortunately, one *really* inspiring example of how we Atheists ought to handle them came to pass just recently. In 2007, a book appeared called *There Is a God: How the World's Most Notorious Atheist Changed His Mind*. And this one wasn't written by just any Dull, but rather by the worst sort imaginable, what You might call a Whittaker Chambers–level traitor to Atheism: the unspeakably treacherous Antony Flew.

You guys know exactly who I'm talking about. Prior to his 2004 declaration that he was a turncoat, Flew, according to the dust jacket, was "probably the best-known atheist in the English-speaking world", whose famous 1950 essay "Theology and Falsification" went on to become "the most widely reprinted philosophical publication of the last half century". That's a lot of Bright capital in one strand of DNA. Even so, did the Flew Judas manage to put a dent on us by turning to Loser?

No, he did not! And the reason why is that Mr. Dawkins—alpha, alpha, alpha! *Grrrr!*—saw the proactive way out. He refers in one cool little footnote to what he calls "the over-publicized tergiversation of the philosopher Antony Flew, who announced in his old age that he had been converted to belief in some sort of deity." I have to admit, I admire the boldness of it. Just like I salivated like an animal over that subsequent *New York Times Magazine* piece, which repeated at *much* greater length exactly what Mr. Dawkins had implied: that Mr. Flew hadn't *really* converted to Christianity. He was just old; falling to pieces; doddering; demographically unfit; just out where the buses don't run.

Yes, that's what Mr. Mark Oppenheimer wrote (and wrote!) in America's best-read Sunday magazine in his "The Turning of an Atheist", which I quote here just a little so You can savor the classiness of the demolition again too:

> With the publication of his new book, Flew is once again talking, and this summer I traveled to England to speak with him. But as I discovered, a conversation with him confuses more than it clarifies. With his powers in decline, Antony Flew, a man who devoted his life to rational argument, has become a mere symbol, a trophy in a battle fought by people whose agendas he does not fully understand.

Now that's what I call a scoop, don't You, guys?

Of course, in the old days, when I myself was a Dull, it would have made my skin crawl to think of stalking an older gentleman to his home and then totally exploiting that opportunity to announce to the world without fear of reproof that he was failing and didn't know what he was talking about. And predictably enough, Roy Abraham Varghese, Mr. Flew's preface writer, did immediately write in to the magazine, like any typical Dull with a sense of decency, to complain about what he called that "contemptible reference".

But those kinds of scruples wouldn't stop us Brights from scoring a point, would they? Right, guys? That's one more thing I love about us! Go, Mr. Oppenheimer, go! I bet he's really, really proud of his work. Even if it was only a beginning, after all. Idea: Let's make lists of every believer over seventy and give them to him for more!

GTG for now, guys. It's group time in here, not my personal favorite. But first, one more piece of good news—that's *gute Nachrichten* in our *Muttersprache*— You'll all really like my next Letter! It's about what I call Atheism's woman problem. And You know what that means—a little more talk about You-know-what!

> TTYL, Your Best Friend Forever
> (and Yours and Yours and Yours),
> A. F. Christian

Todfeinde means "*deadly* enemies", as I just learned in *Deutsch* today. (I told You the attendants gave me a Rosetta Stone set! They said it would help me understand what's happening in here. I sure hope so! Because this is the craziest detox place I've ever seen.)

LETTER SIX
Query: Do Atheists Know Any Women, Children, or Families?

Dearest BFF Atheist Gang,

That's how I'm starting to think about You! Are You all thinking about me that way too? I sure hope so! Because I've *almost* gotten to the part of my story where all You Brights get to find out what made this former Christian into one of You!

Now, before we start today's Letter, which concerns some *super*-important advice about the believers from one who knows *exactly* what You don't about them, a little personal request from Your huge fan here. Do any of You guys have any pull with the Director in this place? If You do, could somebody put in a good word for me?

Number one: I'm trying to get on his good side for obvious reasons (as in, nobody else in here seems to know when they're going to let me out). Number two:

This Director creeps me out. He's not like any other detox head I've ever seen. I don't mind the red cape so much. They're always telling us to find other ways of "expressing ourselves" in these places. So I'm used to that kind of "expressive" thing. But this Director is also a midget. I have a thing about midgets, and not a good one. So if any of You could find out what his plans are and get me out of here sooner rather than later, that would be fantasterrific. And in more ways then *eins*, as we say in *Deutsch* class here.

Moving right along, guys: today's Letter is about one other element of our new Atheism that has me really agitated, because I don't think any of You understand what a liability it is for us Brights.

Perhaps it's because I am a female member of our Species, as so few Brights are. Why do You suppose that is, by the way? Is it an intelligence thing? I won't take it personally if You think I'm inferior (that's *minderwertig* in *Deutsch*). I'm just curious to know what You think.

Anyway, as I was saying before that O.T. bell rang and distracted me again: probably because I am genetically female, not male like all of You and like almost all other Brights, I noticed early on one other reason why we Atheists don't get more converts. The problem is this: most Atheist writing exhibits little knowledge, and even less interest, in certain subsets of our Species that are arguably of numerical and other significance. I'm talking specifically about human children, human women, and human families. In fact, most Atheist writing has little to say about family life or marriage or any of the other institutions historically tied up with reproduction of our Species at all.

Oh, I know what some of You are thinking! Yes, here and there certain subjects that are *related* to families and women and children do come up among the Brights; there's plenty of talk, for example, in the new Atheism (and the old) about the constraints that religion places on "certain behaviors"; there's plenty of mockery of Dulls who *do* think that children and family come first; and as I pointed out in the first Letter, there's lots of Atheist writing, *especially* in that latest round of Your books, about sex and sexuality and sexual repression and other sex stuff.

But the fact remains that Atheists today as yesterday have paid very, very little attention to the human ties that most in our Species are born to and die in—I mean, those of the family. Nobody on our side, and I'm not singling out just You guys here but going back past and including Bertrand Russell and back through the whole history of the Enlightenment, *really* seems to get what it is that drives so many of the believers to Loser—and to church and synagogue and the rest of the sketchy pack—in the first place.

What is that thing? It's the fact that most people live in families, and that most experience religion *through and because of* their family members—father, mother, sister, brother, and the rest of the sentimental bunch. *That's* what Atheist anthropology isn't getting, don't You see? Nobody *really* settles the big issues like You all imply they do—like they're some Ayn Randian *Übermenschen* sitting by themselves in a garret, say; or the last emo scragglebeard left alive on *Lost*, stuck on some mountain someplace and trying to piece out Loser's existence on their lonesome own.

That's why real religious belief becomes so hard to shake, don't You see? It's nothing like one's "individual conscience" or "internal principles" that way. After all, most people can lose *those* pretty easily! Just ask anyone at a party after he's had a few drinks and some ecstasy and 'shrooms.

No, what makes *real* religion so much harder to shake is that a Dull's devotion to Loser never really exists all on its own, apart from everything else where it might be easily plucked from him. Instead, it's stuck waaaaay down inside, all wrapped up like some diabolical double helix with the other *people* in his life. That makes quitting an awfully hard thing to do. It's like trying to stop four antidepressants at once instead of just one, if You know what I mean: don't try it on Your own!

Some of the Dulls, for example, come to believe in Loser for one kind of family reason—say, because they love their husbands or wives too much to believe that death really cuts the two apart forever. Even more people—*way* more, from what this former Christian has seen—are drawn to belief because they feel that way about their *brats*. They think in the craziest way that there's something infinite about their love for their children, something that transcends these finite shackles of our cells—and they infer from that powerful feeling that love really is stronger than death, as their stupid old book says somewhere.

Now You might not think that this gross sentimentality is much of a force in the great Natural scheme of things. But I'm here to tell You that it is. It's familial love that first gives people the idea of infinite love. It's that kind of love that puts them in touch with Loser in the first place—meaning that nothing, really, is more of a problem for our side than the existence of human families.

And this former Christian should know! When I lived in a family myself, I was a textbook Dull. And when I went off on my own, especially after those four babelicious years at the university, I started wavering. Oh, I'd go to church here and there, all right, especially if Mom called from home to ask if I was getting there. *Then* I'd slink off and usually be late.

But when I *really* didn't want to get out of bed, and there was *really* no one around who knew or cared whether I did, I got into exactly that habit that we Brights have raised to an art form. I'd tell myself that my avoidance of Loser was all about one (high-minded!) thing, when it was *really* about something else and not remotely elevated. You know, like when we Brights say things like, "The Thomistic doctrine of transubstantiation of essences is too contra-Newtonian to be countenanced by the twenty-first century"—when what we *really* mean is, "What the hell; why should I waste an hour in church when all it's going to do is remind me of rules I'd just as soon forget?"

You guys know just what I mean here! To take another example: it's like when people say, "There's no Logic to the efficacy of prayer and divine intervention in linear space and time"—when what they *really* mean is, "I don't *care* if she's young enough to be my daughter; I'm going to have sex with her in a heartbeat if I get the chance." That kind of Atheist self-deception thing! Yes, that's what I learned to do too as soon as I didn't have a family around to remind me of self-sacrifice and birth and death and other things tied up with religion that make no sense when You live by and for Yourself. That was the beginning of my road to You.

And later in life, ditto that. By the time I met Lobo in rehab and we started living together in New York following his record five days of staying clean (what a dork—I beat him by almost a week!), I had almost stopped thinking about church and Loser entirely. I admit, thanks to Lobo I was also taking enough drugs after a while to make me forget my own Facebook password. But two, and more important, we were both nowhere near what You could call a family, unless You count his hepcat divorced dad, who hit on me once when Lobo was out. And Loser knows that neither of us had any intention of starting a family of our own, either. That's what I'm trying to explain here. *That's* the kind of situation that's fertile grounds for Atheism.

Now let me be very clear here in the most constructive way possible, like Simon on *American Idol* when he's *secretly* rooting for one contestant but has to be critical-seeming at the same time to get across what the contestant will have to do to please buzzing gnat-brain Paula and talking Sequoia stump Randy to survive into the next round of the show. Just so You know, I *personally* couldn't care less about the Dulls and their domestic so-called lives—especially their lame monogamous sex lives and their cheesy little kids. I'm so *over* that, as You'll soon see.

Similarly, I personally couldn't agree with You more that the believers' idea of what a "family" is—mother, father, and their litter—is fully as retarded as any of the *many* other things the "Church" has been wrong about, as well as causing more human misery than practically anything else Humans have devised before or since—with the possible exception, of course, of something called Antabuse (little rehab joke!). And since I *personally* am also never going to reproduce, there is not even a hint of sentimental slop clouding my judgment here. I say all that so You know that I'm as realistic about this business of human children and their place in Nature's pecking order as any other Bright.

But You see, in failing to deal with the reality that most people are going to have these putrid "families" of theirs, and what having those "families" does to the inner wiring of the average Dull, You Brights all are missing something important about how the religion racket gets transferred in the first place. This problem may account for more of the hemorrhage to Christianity, especially, than You may realize. I'm not saying the Dulls have Reason on their side, of course. Like so much else that motivates them, the elevation of their offspring to some kind of extra-Species status is preposterous. But it's families that make people religious, not vice versa.

Let's throw in a little contest here to illustrate my point. Which view of human children resonates more with the average parent—our side, or that of the Dulls?

For the Dull side, we'll pick as a contestant that so-called Cold War intellectual Whittaker Chambers. He's a total tool, I know, as well as a majoroso traitor to Atheism;

but he has his uses here. And for representing the Atheist side, we'll pick the author of *Christopher Hitchens Is Great* or whatever that book of his was called.

Here we go then! As Mr. Hitchens notes in His book, Chambers, a Dull convert, described in his memoir *Witness* one particular moment that helped turn him to Christianity, namely, studying the ear of his infant daughter. Said Chambers:

My daughter was in her high chair. I was watching her eat. She was the most miraculous thing that had ever happened in my life. I liked to watch her even when she smeared porridge on her face or dropped it meditatively on the floor. My eye came to rest on the delicate convolutions of her ear—those intricate, perfect ears.

The thought passed through my mind: "No, those ears were not created by any chance coming together of atoms in nature (the Communist view). They could only have been created by immense design."

The thought was involuntary and unwanted. I crowded it out of my mind. But I never wholly forgot it or the occasion. I had to crowd it out of my mind. If I had completed it, I should have had to say: Design presupposes God. I did not

86

then know that, at that moment, the finger of God was first laid upon my forehead.

I know, gag *me* with a spoon too; the passage reeks of mawkish poor reasoning like so much else in Dull literature. And yet I confess: upon reading that passage in Chambers for the first time, way before I ever ascended to Atheism, I too resonated with his point. It seemed just like the sort of thing I'd have said of my own hypothetical daughter if I'd stopped to think about it.

You see, it's just very, very difficult for most mothers and fathers to look at their children and to understand as we Brights do that those creatures are randomly assembled confections of molecules and limbs that have been adapting willy-nilly since the lungfish. That just isn't how most people feel about their babies and children—*ever*. I know this from watching my friends who have kids. I even know it if I *really* zero in on my hypothetical daughter (let's call her H.D. for short). And H.D. is just virtual, You know! But anyone who stops to think about it can see the problem for us Atheists here. Most parents love their children with a love they experience as infinite—and that glimpse of the infinite, *exactly* as in the case of aesthetics, sends them running toward Loser.

Certainly Mr. Hitchens' response to Chambers is unhelpful to us! Here's how He frames the Atheist take: "I too", He writes, have marveled at the sweet little ears of my female offspring, but never without noticing that (a) they always need a bit of a clean-out, (b) that they look mass-produced even when set against the inferior ears of other people's daughters, (c) that as people get older their ears look more and more absurd from behind, and (d) that much lower animals, such as cats and bats, have much more fascinating and lovely and more potent ears.

Now there are two problems with this kind of Atheist ridicule of Mr. Chambers' point, it seems to me. One is that if we put it to the *parents* of the world that upon studying their daughters' ears they are to choose whose response they like best, Mr. Hitchens is going to lose hands down. His alternative just comes off as cold-blooded (I mean that figuratively, not literally, of course). I'm not saying that's what should happen. Just that *most* people who reproduce, *most* of the time, think their own children are somehow precious, "created", and they don't think they are inferior in any way to bats and cats and other mammals, let alone to creatures from elsewhere on the genus tree.

None of which means the little twerps are. Again, I hold no brief for *real* children at all. Like any other thinking Atheist, my desire to see my DNA continued is no match for my desire to avoid anyone younger and fitter than I am!

Now, in the *total* spirit of constructive criticism, I think I've figured out why we Brights have this weakness. It's because a good many Atheists, both historically and today, have been childless or otherwise living outside real families themselves. Look at Spinoza, sometimes called the first Atheist philosopher. Look at big swinging Forebear Nietzsche. Or look at our *especially* fabulous Enlightenment ancestor Jean-Jacques Rousseau.

Oops! I forgot; Rousseau *did* have kids. *But* He sent all five of them to an orphanage as soon as they were born so they wouldn't interfere with His work (kind of like the sleepover version of what busy moms and dads do today). According to historians, they almost certainly all died there at an early age. So under the circs I think we can safely loophole Rousseau in among the childless Brights, if that's okay with You. (Kind of gives a new meaning to "man, born free, is everywhere in chains", doesn't it? No wonder He thought that one up. Talk about trying things at home!)

And just as we Brights are vulnerable to the charge of not knowing anything about children, so do we have a related problem: human women. Now, I've read through each and every one of Your books; I've studied each and every YouTube clip I could find; I've even Google-alerted everybody's names so that nothing about this new Atheism gets away from me. And what I can't find, anywhere, is any mention of this empirical fact: across the world, in every religion and not just among the Dulls, women are far more likely than men to keep Loser's institutions going strong—more likely to attend church (or whatever), more likely to pray, more likely to indoctrinate their spawn into the same rituals, and so blubbery on.

Now don't You all think that's an important fact? And even more important, why do You think it *is* a fact? Because it seems to me that there can only be one of two explanations for this gender difference: either females really are intellectually deficient compared to males or something about the way they live gives them ideas that men don't have.

Again, I blame the kids. Maybe something about taking care of smaller and weaker members of the Species makes it easier for females to imagine that someone stands in that same sort of loving relationship to *them*. Or maybe the experience of loving something more than they ever thought possible makes them think that some extra-human love might be out there for them too. Who knows? I'm not explaining here, just saying that *some* explanation of the female role in keeping religion going seems called for—and You guys haven't even touched it.

Either that or we double-XXers really *are* all dumb as dirt! Do You guys secretly suspect that might be true? If that's what You think, why don't You just come out and say so? I mean, it's not like Brights are squeamish about a lot of other things we believe—as You will see in my next two Letters, where I quote *really* interesting things from some of the classics of our genre!

In sum, the incontrovertible fact is that human families, and especially the ties between women and children, are the chief enemies of Atheism. I'm just saying this so You know I don't claim to have all the solutions here! All I know as a former Dull is where the problems are. (Did You know, by the way, that the German word for "solution" is *Lösung*, which is really an awful lot like *Loser*? How ironic is that?!)

You've all been patient long enough, so *very* soon I'm going to stop with the criticism and all this talk of what we Brights have done wrong and turn instead to what has been done soooooooooo right, that is, the beginning of my turn to You!

Proactively Yours! *Es ist ein Kampf bis auf Messer!** And if anyone does talk to the Director, can You ask him what the heck kind of rehab uses German as occupational therapy in the first place? Thanks, guys!

Smoochies,
A. F. Christian

*"It's a fight to the finish!"

LETTER SEVEN
The Unbelievably Annoying Problem of Christian Moral High Ground

Dear Distinguished Atheist Friends (that's *Lieber Herren Doktoren Atheisten Freunde* in *Deutsch*),

Hi, everybody! It's A. F. Christian here, reporting again from the front with some more *super*-informed advice for our new Atheist Movement!

First up today, an exciting little announcement: as of this seventh Letter—that's today's—we're about 70 percent through with my story about how this former Christian converted to Atheism. Isn't that *great*? Now, on the other hand, that means there are still three more Letters to come after this one. And what *that* means is, writing in and complaining at *this* point that people don't understand the plot here is kind of unfair. It's like getting two-thirds of the way through an episode of *House*, and calling up Hugh Laurie to complain that he hasn't thought of Wegener's granulomatosis or Behcet's syndrome or Takayasu's arteritis yet! And who jumps the gun like that? How about nobody!

So please, just as if this were TV or YouTube, hang in there, folks! As those readers who *have* been following along know already, it's not like the Letters are heavy lifting. They're not some excruciosaurus brain-busting treatise about Loser, or anything else. They just tell a little *story*, which is about what led me away from religion and toward our phenomenal godlessness. I'm sure everybody will find out in the end about whatever loose end in the story they're wondering about—like why I'm taking Rosetta Stone German, how I ended up in this crazy rehab run by the midget Director with the red cape, what finally happened with my big zero of a boyfriend, Lobo, and the rest of the details about my turn to Atheism. By the end of the series You'll know all this and more, and no one will get a migraine getting from here to there, I pinky swear. Okeydokey, guys?

Now back to serious Atheist business!

Today's subject concerns an idea that is absolutely *critical* to the success of our godlessness, namely, how the believers' capture of the moral high ground on certain issues—in particular, what they call the "life issues"—continues to deprive us Atheists of the converts we deserve. I'll start by discussing the particular leading "life" issue where they've left us Brights in the P.R. dust: abortion.

Now, let's begin by noticing that there *is* such a thing as an Atheist position on abortion—namely, that just about every Bright in history or currently in print is in favor of it. At first, I have to admit, I didn't quite get why everybody should be so North-Korean-election lopsided about this. After all, we Atheists are supposed to be Freethinkers. We do disagree about some important things, like—well, like nothing I can think of offhand, but I'm sure there's *something* we don't all think alike about, somewhere. This issue isn't one of them, though. You can scour almost all contemporary works on our side and find not a molecule of difference on the question of the morality of abortion.

It's funny, isn't it? Because even as recently as a few generations ago, at least a *couple* of people were apparently able to be Atheists and antiabortion at the same time. For example, two of the few influential female Atheists in history, Susan B. Anthony and Elizabeth Cady Stanton, were exactly that. Even our spiritual antimother Margaret Sanger was apparently conflicted about the morality of abortion—or at least about abortions committed by white people. (Don't worry! I would not *ordinarily* bring Margaret Sanger's name into *anything*, at least not around the Dulls aware of Her work. We all know what a liability Her flamboyant racism can be.) For whatever reason, though, it appears that this kind of dissent in Atheist thought just quit evolving.

By now, being anti-Loser is pretty much a proxy for being proabortion, and usually vice versa too.

Now, there seem to be two arguments for abortion on which today's Brights unanimously agree. The first, which is simple enough, goes like this: religious people, and *only* religious people, are against abortion; religious people are misled, and usually stupid; therefore, being against abortion is not something a Bright should be.

Personally, just between us, I wouldn't make too much of that one, at least in public. I'm not sure it would survive Logical dissection. I'm just putting it out for consideration, because it appears in so many of Your books. That's what You might call the back-story syllogism for abortion in today's Atheism.

The front-story case for abortion is a little more sophisticated, and also pops up all the time, occasionally with words like "utilitarianism" or "consequentialism" thrown in alongside. It goes like this: the embryo/fetus cannot feel; *therefore* anything we do to it is fine.

Thus, for example, Mr. Dawkins asks, "Does an embryo suffer?" and answers, "Presumably not if it is aborted before it has a nervous system; and even if it is old enough to have a nervous system it surely suffers less, than, say, an adult cow in a slaughterhouse." Similarly, Mr. Harris explains that "many of us consider human fetuses in the first trimester to be more or less like rabbits: having imputed to them a range of happiness and suffering that does not grant them full status in our moral community." Mr. Hitchens—who once was rumored to harbor subversive (i.e., antiabortion) tendencies on this issue—seems to have abandoned any such qualms. In His latest book, He makes another point that Atheists often invoke to justify abortion, i.e., the fact that it also occurs Naturally:

> There may be many circumstances in which it is not desirable to carry a fetus to full term. Either nature or god appears to appreciate this, since a very large number of pregnancies are "aborted," so to speak, because of malformations, and are politely known as "miscarriages." Sad though this is, it is probably less miserable an outcome than the vast number of deformed or idiot children who would otherwise have been born, or stillborn, or whose brief lives would have been a torment to themselves and others. As with evolution in general, therefore, in utero we see a microcosm of nature and evolution itself.

Now let me please count the ways—as gently as I can, and *hopefully* without anyone pounding out an e-mail who hasn't even finished this Letter yet!—in which I think we Atheists are making mistakes both tactical and strategic on this critical subject.

Number one: As a matter of Logic, the argument that "Nature aborts lots of embryos, and therefore it's fine if people do too", is really embarrassingly absurd. I don't want to offend anyone, but considering all the brainpower we Brights lay claim to, it's amazing that nobody has thought to correct that particular howler. After all, if Nature floods half of Indonesia without warning, does that mean it's okay for people to do it too? Am I okay on running over my neighbor just because car accidents are the leading cause of death in some Species age groups? You see where I'm going with this: nowhere good for us.

Number two, and *very* important: We must *not* let Mr. Harris or any other Bright, ever again, compare the unborn human DNA clump to a "rabbit". Danger, OOOO-GA! We could call it a "rat", possibly, or maybe a "naked mole rat"—or what's probably best, just stick to the Scientific-sounding "fetus". But "rabbit" or other mammalian cutie, never! Nobody wants anything bad to happen to one of *them*. Even a six-year-old will tell You that it's wrong to take apart an unborn bunny rabbit!

Third, and here I'll give You inside information as only a former Dull could: It really worries me that today's Atheists just don't get what the pro-lifers are about. I know what You're objecting, I know! Yes, all those recent Atheist books do talk about the murderer who bombed an abortion clinic. And that's exactly my point. That's all *any* of today's Atheists talk about when they talk about the pro-life movement. And that is a very *dangerous* mistake that risks putting off countless Dulls who know better—because that clinic bomber is not the real face of the pro-life movement at all.

Who is? Well, have any of You ever seen one of the rallies in Washington, D.C., on the anniversary of our favorite Bright decision ever, *Roe v. Wade*? (I'm guessing not!) I have. I went several times with my Dull friends, back before I met Lobo and stopped talking to Loser. And I'm here to tell You that unfortunately for us guys who want to protect the so-called right to abortion at all costs, those pro-life rallies on the Mall every January are *nothing* like the rallies that the pro-abortion people stage. You know those *other* rallies, I'm sure—the ones full of grim ladies well past aborting age, marching with coat hangers as their emblems, yelling about their "right" to end the pregnancies they'll never again have.

No, the pro-lifers and *their* rallies are a different world altogether. There are children, families, and teenagers *everywhere*. There are kids playing Frisbee. Kids holding hands. Kids horsing around and shoving each other. Kids with earrings and tattoos. Kids with rosaries. Kids wearing T-shirts that read, "I'm adopted and thanks, Mom, for having me." Kids, kids, kids, kids, *kids*—are

You getting the horrible drift here? It's more like a rave or a rock concert than an ordinary political event—I mean it *would* be, only the kids are a lot more healthy-looking and there aren't any drugs, of course.

I cannot emphasize enough how *seriously bad* it is for us Atheists that the face of the pro-life movement is a *youthful* face. And what do You think pulls all those kids into the pro-life scene? I know You will say indoctrination; but at the risk of annoying everybody all over again, I have to say as a former Christian that You're wrong. Those kids are in the movement for the same reason that the civil-rights marchers—who are *their* rock stars—also took to the streets: because they're totally convinced that in taking a stand against abortion, they're doing something good for the world.

Why *is* that? Don't You ever wonder?

I have, and I think the answer has to do with something we Atheists—and plenty of our Secular allies too—just don't get yet. It's this: *living around the fact of abortion on demand has changed some people, and the closer they get to the ground, as it were, the more seriously they take it.*

I mean, face it! If You're over fifty, there's not much chance that anyone would have aborted *You*. But nowadays it's different. It's like anyone who's even *born* now, in the Age of Choice, either requires explanation or feels like there's a reason for it. It's changed the existential experience of the very question, *Why am I here?*

I'm not saying this bizarre state of affairs is alto-gether bad for our godlessness. Some kids, today as ever, *do* turn effortlessly toward Atheism's chief transmitter belts among the young, i.e., nihilism and melancholy. In fact, some do it easier than ever. The fact that their generation is the first truly disposable one—even *disposed-of* one—puts extra pressure on *all* of today's kids to find a meaning in life. Some just can't. That's what Goth is for. And a lot of their music. And Norplant. And, of course, drugs.

But other kids, including many of the more serious kids, get pulled instead by those same questions toward Loser. When *those* kids look at those pictures at the rallies, they don't see what nonbelievers see—a mistake of Nature "fixed" somehow by violent human interven-tion. No, they see something else—what their baby sister looked like four years ago on the sonogram, what they themselves were not very long ago. They see them-selves. They see their friends. They see their *siblings*. And all of this propels them away from us, and toward the people who tell them this thing is wrong—people concentrated for one reason or another on Loser's side.

So many of us Brights just don't get this part of the struggle! I'm not blaming anybody in particular here. I think it's one more generational thing. As in my first Letter, where I tried to explain what You all are miss-ing about the Sexual Revolution—like its unhappy consequences for lots of people—I'm trying here to explain something similar. Most young Dulls do not think abortion is *an* issue; they think it is *the* issue that proves their Christian morality to be superior. I cannot emphasize this point enough: millions of them *are* Dulls just because of abortion on demand. They believe—as that hideously erudite enemy of ours Hadley Arkes wrote—that abortion is "the central moral issue of our day, the issue from which everything else radiates".

Is anybody still not getting it? A great many of the believers do not think abortion is wrong because Loser *tells* them it's wrong (though he does, of course). They think it's wrong *in the first place*—and when they look around to see who else does too, and who *exactly* speaks up against this and other quote unquote inhuman transgressions as the Dulls see them (more on those in the next Letter), what they see are the institutions speaking in Loser's name.

And *just like that* do many Dulls get drawn into those religious places: not because they particularly want to! Not because forking over money and getting up early on Sunday and getting laughed at in all the best places is their idea of fun, either! But because, when they go looking for what they consider to be their stupid old moral high ground, those institutions are the only ones left standing on it.

You guys know me by now! I'm not saying the pathetic do-gooding cheek-turners are right! In fact, I for one understand *exactly* how important the practice of abortion on demand is to our cause of spreading Atheism. As I pointed out in the last Letter, human families, and *especially* the ties between human women and their children, are the chief enemies of godlessness. If it weren't for families, many people would never get the idea of eternal love—that critical stepping-stone toward Loserland—in the first place. Severing those ties at the root, quite literally, is therefore something that our Atheism must be allowed to do.

But to do it, we're going to need arguments—so it doesn't help that we've failed to capture any high ground for ourselves on the issue. Yes, I know that some Brights have tried! Mr. Harris says, for instance, that "if you are worried about human suffering, abortion should rank very low on your list of concerns." He even tells the Christians that "your efforts to constrain the sexual behavior of consenting adults—and even to discourage your own sons and daughters from having premarital sex— are almost never geared toward the relief of human suffering. In fact, relieving suffering seems to rank rather low on your list of priorities."

And here again, we Atheists are blowing it. Many of the Dulls object to abortion *precisely* because of what Mr. Harris rules out: *because it causes suffering*. I'm not even talking about the suffering of the fetus here, but of the suffering it can cause *other* people too. (Ever heard of Project Rachel? Yikes!) Nobody on our side seems to see what those packs of teenagers on the Mall every January understand without my having to write them Letters every week—that there's a connection between the practice of abortion on demand and human damage, one that keeps millions of people away from our glorious godlessness *just on account of that*.

In closing, I'm just going to throw atcha a series of questions that I think we and future converts—I mean, if anyone else besides me is going to become an Atheist convert—really need to address here:

Number one, and whether anyone believes it or not, can we Brights please get someone out front on the idea that Atheists can be pro-life too? (Not Mr. Hitchens again; He flip-flops.) Just to confuse at least some of the Dulls? So they don't think they *must* have religion to be against this thing? That might really help.

Sonography: How can we Atheists get rid of it? Or at least make it harder to get at? It's been nothing less than one big conveyer belt to that old debbil, the Christian moral high ground, ever since its diabolical, as it were, invention.

Every time a pregnant woman watches that screen, we risk losing a potential convert. And even when it's deployed to make more abortions, the score is still *way* lopsided. The sex-selection abortions in India and China and elsewhere don't *begin* to make up for what we're losing at home.

Again under the heading of protecting ourselves from attack, even if no one means it: we Brights have *got* to drop the argument that goes, "So what; abortion isn't the same as first-degree murder." It's killing us out there (as it were).

After all, when does something have to be first-degree murder to be *wrong*? Is this really what we want people to think Atheism stands for? It may be exactly what some Brights actually think, and I respect that. But do we really want to broadcast it to our enemies? Do You know how much fun the "theocons" alone could have with *that* little slip?

I know what You're all thinking, and You know I'm with You! Even as we confuse our enemies by acting as if there's room for dissent about this, we should also ratchet up the rhetoric in favor of abortion. What do we have to be defensive about, anyway? As if a few weeks or months here or there should make any abortion controversial, ever! And how about the damage Hillary and others do to us (I'm assuming tongue in cheek) when they say, "Safe, legal, and rare." Why "rare"? That makes it sound like the Dulls have a point! Why not "Abortion in America: Safe, legal, and lots"?! Now that's more like it! Do You guys think we can get any support for *that*?

Okay, maybe not. But if anyone has other proactive ideas, let me know!

Your pal among pals,
A. F. Christian

LETTER EIGHT
My Turn to Atheism, Part One: From Baby Killers to Barnyard Mayhem

To All My Awesome Leading Atheist Idols,

Hey there again! This is one Letter I know everyone's been waiting for—Part One of the sincerious tale of my personal evolutionary leap into Atheism. I'm soooooo excited to be getting to this part of the story, everybody! Isn't it *sweet*? It's like that moment on *Project Runway* where the one designer guy who made a dress has been dissed by the judges and goes off to cry, and then the other designer guy also gets his dress dissed by the judges too and he goes off to cry too, and then there's no one left standing but the winner who's a female for *once*—and then *all* the judges come out on the runway to hug her and tell her how fabulous her dress design is and how much better it is than anyone else's. And she cries too, because she's *soooooo* happy that they're happy with her! Just like we're all going to do when I get through with these Letters! I can hardly wait till we're all there like that, can You?

So enough with all this depressing (if helpful!) talk in my first seven Letters about what today's Atheism has done wrong. Now let's look instead at what it's done *right*—so right that it turned this former Christian Dull into godless Bright convert *numero uno*. And to get there, I'll need to take You just a little ways back in time to my final days as a believer and explain what happened next.

As I mentioned earlier, my personal religious belief took the usual battering by Atheists and their fellow travelers when I went off to college. What was left of it then got further blown away by my idiotosaurus boyfriend Lobo (about whom You'll hear more in my next Letter than You ever wanted to, but it can't be helped). So what with one thing and another, by the age of twenty-one I'd abandoned most of the religion I'd grown up with, and become what You might call a classic "cafeteria" Dull.

Actually, I would have been more accurately described as an *anorexic* cafeteria Dull, considering how little was left on my religious plate by then. Like any other believer in name only, I thought that I could somehow have it all, theologically speaking—You know, jettisoning whatever I didn't like about Loser (especially those laws about You-know-what!) and keeping whatever doctrines I

107

"personally" approved of (i.e., the ones that sounded good and didn't really get in my face).

But of those few remaining things about Christianity that I *did* approve, I really felt more strongly than most Atheists might imagine. What finally made me proud to be a Dull, what *really* lay beneath my unwillingness to relinquish all that nonsense, was that I thought Loser and his followers had stood—and stood uniquely—against some of the grosser practices of human history.

Abortion, infanticide, pedophilia, bestiality, human sacrifice—these were things that I then thought of as somehow beneath the dignity of our Species. The fact that Judaism and Christianity had set their faces against these things was powerfully appealing to me—and not only to me, of course, but to millions of other people across the ages too. As that überpapist Elizabeth Anscombe said somewhere, it was a "known fact that Christianity drew people out of the pagan world, always saying no to these things."

And though I'm embarrassed to admit it now, there were probably also personal reasons for my vulnerability. Perhaps because I am a female, for example, it wasn't hard to peer back through time to the hills of Rome and feel creeped out by the thought of the *patria potestas* law, which granted fathers a right to off any unwanted baby girls. What kind of gynophobe brutocracy does that, I used to wonder? It seemed obvi to me then, as it does to so many Dulls now, that a society in which the weakest were getting hosed so ruthlessly could use a little moral fine-tuning—and that Christianity with all its sins at least had a fork for that kind of thing.

Ditto, I was freaked about the female infanticide under way in our own time. It seemed crazy to me—then, anyway—that all this preemptive baby killing was going on with no shout-out whatsoever from Western feminists or other Progressive types. Weren't any of them female too? Why weren't they bug-eyed like me about those weird statistics from China and India and a few other places, showing that ratios of XY chromosomes to XX ones were getting seriously out of whack?

Euthanasia to me was another no-brainer, also for personal reasons. I'd been a patient one too many times myself! So I didn't think it was the most brilliant idea to ask someone who's flat on his back with enough drugs packed inside to open a pharmacy to pay attention and decide whether he wants to live or die. Plus, the whole idea of a life not worth living seemed sketchy to me. When You got right down to it, I thought, having healthy people wipe out sick people just didn't seem fair—not unless we were going to let both parties flip coins each time so the patient had at least a shot at telling the attendant that it was *his* turn to be offed instead. But nobody I knew of seemed to be advocating *that*.

My personal aversion to human sacrifice: same old, same old. I'd actually been to Mexico. I'd seen the creepy pyramids at Teotihuacán and the architectural models of how they looked in the old days, accessorized with tens of thousands of human skulls. I'd seen the well at Chichén Itzá whose bottom is full of children's bones, and the sacrificial stones You can find all over Central America—You know, the ones helpfully carved with gulleys from the center to the side to make the blood run down faster. Nobody could tell me, at least not back then, that Christianity wasn't *some* kind of step up from all that. I can't stand that Loserholic G. K. Chesterton any more than other Brights can, but I have to admit, he nailed the moral-equivalency quackery down: "There is a very real sense in which the Christian is worse than the heathen, the Spaniard worse than the Red Indian, or even the Roman potentially worse than the Carthaginian. But there is only one sense in which he is worse; and that is not in being positively worse. The Christian is only worse because it is his business to be better."

But at the same time—and here we get to the very heart of my turn!—despite clinging to Christianity *just* on account of its belief in something called human dignity, there was something key I wasn't getting. You see, I didn't *really* believe in what the other Dulls called the slippery slope. I didn't really think that if You just

110

got rid of Loser, the world would bit by bit become anything-goes. The Dulls were always saying such things, and I'd always nod when they did. But deep down inside, I thought that was just some easily led histrionic exaggeration thing. I didn't *really* think any of the consequences they talked about would happen.

Oh, I knew about a few teensy-weensy historical problems for institutionalized Atheism here and there! You know, what the believers call major assaults on human dignity—like certain things about the French Revolution, say; or those unfortunate excesses of Social *Darwinismus* during certain decades in *Deutschland* in the twentieth century; or like the history of Communism, period. I even knew about the scholarly trial balloons here and there in our own time that seemed to other people to prove beyond a doubt that there *was* a slippery slope—like the ACLU's defenses of child pornography, say, or like Peter Singer's reopening of the question of whether offing human babies is always wrong.

But deep down inside, again, I *believed* You Atheist guys when You said that if we just ditched Loser, the world would still be left with some kind of Humanist "morality". And that was exactly why I didn't jump ship for Atheism any sooner than I did, You see. After all, I thought, if we're all going to be stuck with rules and laws and morality no matter what, what's the point of leaving one worthless old system for another? It's like saying You have to choose between Stoli and Grey Goose, when they're both doing the same thing! Why bother making the trade? That's what I thought back then, during my very last days as a Dull.

And then something really incredible happened: by actually reading some of what our fellow Atheists and fellow travelers were writing—a stack of unbelievably eye-popping items handed over to me by Lobo, for reasons I'll explain in the next Letter—I realized something that changed my life: *the Dulls were right about the existence of that slope, and I was wrong.*

Exhibit A, You might say, was something that fellow Bright Steven Pinker published in the Sunday *New York Times* a few years back. Titled "Why They Kill Their Newborns", this essay explained what I once would have thought inexplicable. For contrary to what the Dulls have been saying for two thousand years, Pinker made the point that infanticide was in some brain-bending sense *normal*. "It's hard to maintain that neonaticide [baby killing] is an illness", he explained, "when we learn that it has been practiced and accepted in most cultures throughout history."

Now at first, I have to admit, I didn't quite get this Logic; after all, disease and infections of every kind have also been rampant throughout human societies, and that fact hasn't led physicians to redefine disease and infections as healthy. But then I realized that this much was just the setup. His actual point was nothing less than proof positive that the Dulls were right about the slippery slope. For it was the *abortion debate*, the author explained, that showed just how hard it is to decide when "personhood"—in effect, a right to live—began. And just as any given month is arbitrary before birth, so too is some unspecified amount of time that follows it. "Neonaticide", he explained, "forces us to examine even that boundary [of birth]." In that case, he asks, "How do you provide grounds for outlawing neonaticide?" His answer: *"The facts don't make it easy* [italics mine, not His]."

Wow! Using the fact of abortion on demand to make us rethink the morality of infanticide: what more proof of the slippery slope could one possibly want? But as it turned out, and as I found out reading further in Lobo's stack of papers, plenty more was out there—including in some pretty unexpected places. For instance, when Daniel Patrick Moynihan coined the phrase "defining deviancy down", he probably wasn't thinking of the family farm. But somebody else sure was!

For it turned out that yet another Bright, the aforementioned Princeton professor Peter Singer, published an essay in 2001 arguing for a bold new take on one more behavior banned by Judeo-Christian theology. This was the classic entitled "Heavy Petting". Despite the ongoing collapse of many former taboos, the professor wrote there, not *all* of them have crumbled; no, at least one—"sex with animals"—remains. Moreover, he blamed that taboo right on Loser himself—because "especially in the Judeo-Christian tradition ... we have always seen ourselves as distinct from animals, and imagined that a wide, unbridgeable gulf separates us from them."

Let's just say that closing up that gulf, to put it politely, is just what the rest of his essay is all about! At the risk of TMI, I have to say there's stuff in there about chickens. And an octopus. And about "occasionally mutually satisfying activities" that "may develop" with Your favorite canine. I can't quote anything else, or the Director might not let me send this. But Red Rover, Red Rover! Don't let Professor come over!

Talk about being roused from Your dogmatic slumber! (Little joke there.) At first, I have to admit, I didn't really get this one either. In fact, at *first*, I thought the professor was sneakily proving a rather unpopular point made by the "Church"—that when human sexuality is amputated from reproductive possibility, plenty of weird things are going to happen, and some of them are really going to stink. You know that thing the believers call *reductio ad absurdum*, where You prove how lame an idea is by riffing off a particularly bad Logical consequence of it? *That's* what I thought he was up to—as I say, at first. But no.

So doing the Atheist math as my reading suggested it: if abortion *already* had been normalized in post-Christian circles, and infanticide was in the *process* of being normalized in those same places, and even bestiality was getting the Princeton University seal of approval, what evidence could *possibly* be added to prove that the Christians were right about that slippery slope?

Well, how about this: nothing less than an attack on the very idea of human dignity, *period*.

And that, which we might call Exhibit C, is exactly what Professor Steven Pinker published in 2009 in *The New Republic*. And he further did it under the title—no, I am *not* making this up as if his piece is a satire that I just stuck in here to prove the point, because it's totally serious—"The Stupidity of Dignity".

The essay's main target was Leon Kass—one of the most hard-core serious Loser-enablers out there, as You probably all know. Do You recall that he chaired something called the President's Council on Bioethics? From that post Kass advanced any number of Dull-friendly positions, all in the name of human dignity—like always reminding how we're not supposed to perform certain experiments on people, or what's wrong with creating fetuses and carving them up for spare parts, or how after certain misadventures in the 1930s and 1940s it's become even more imperative to remember that all Humans have intrinsic worth—yes, even the unfit ones—and related Dull-sounding superstitions like that.

And Pinker, bless His soul (sorry for the slip!), won't have any of it! As He explains, dignity is an "almost" useless concept. It's "relative, fungible, and often harmful". It's only "skin-deep". The "sin of theocon ethics" is exactly this faith in a sweeping claim to dignity—through which the believers hope to "stage-manage" social change. It seeks to impose "a Catholic agenda on a secular democracy" by using "dignity"—those are the professor's skeptical quotations around that word, not mine—to "condemn anything that gives someone the creeps". (Hey, I didn't know Kass was a Catholic! Did You? Ha, ha!)

I really can't quite explain to everybody the effect of all this Bright light on this particular Dull, who was clinging to Loser by the barest threads anyway. As Keats swooned on first looking into Chapman's Homer, as Dr. Dre must have thought when he first saw Eminem, so did I feel as if my very DNA were being resequenced as I devoured and redevoured Lobo's package of texts. And putting together one thing and another—the ongoing normalization of all those things Loser said was wrong, the attack on the very idea of human dignity itself—I realized finally that the believers in all their woolly-headedness were right. Everything really *would* be permitted if we just sent Loser packing; it was only a matter of time.

116

I know what You're thinking, and You're right too! It's a twisted kind of outcome for my story. After all, many a querulous Catholic or Mormon or Lutheran or Jew has been *confirmed* in his religious belief just by realizing what I realized then. In fact, many a believer *is* a believer exactly because of connecting those dots between Atheism and the return of pagan morals, and inferring from them that Loser is right. But I, for reasons You will see in full in the next Letter, was no ordinary Christian by then. What most Dulls would have called "vindication" spelled something entirely different for me: namely, *Freedom* with a capital *F*.

And so concludes Part One of my turn to Atheism— with the realization that contrary to what I'd clung to in Christianity, nothing—no, nothing at all—*really* is beneath a human male or female (with the occasional exception for some of the family pet).

And *that* revelation, for reasons everyone will understand when You read my next Letter—which tells the whole demented story of Lobo, me, some stale Little Debbie oatmeal cookies, the Friday night party that landed me here, and all the other details about my turn to Atheism (Part Two)—was the best news I'd personally gotten in a long, long time.

Yours "woof" waiting for (get it? LOL!),
A. F. Christian

117

LETTER NINE
My Turn to Atheism, Part Two:
An Internet Café in Portland, the Little
Debbie Tea Party, and You

Dearest Fellow Brights among Brights,

Drum roll, all You leading Atheist guys—this finally is it! The moment everybody's been waiting for. Part Two of the true facts in the actual chronological sequence of what *exactly* turned this former Christian to godlessness!

I've just got to share with You before starting today: this place is the craziest rehab I've ever seen. I mean, I knew I'd end up someplace serious after what happened that night two months ago. But *here*? If those whiners on *Intervention* could see *this* detox, they'd never touch anything stronger than Red Bull again!

As mentioned, for example, the Director here is a midget who wears a red cape. And even though I've talked to him like twenty times, I've never really seen his face, because he keeps the hood up. His assistants were the ones who gave me Rosetta Stone German, You know. They said studying it would help me understand Atheism. And then for no reason at all today, one of those creepy attendants of his took away my whole language kit—no explanation, no apologies, no nothing! They said the Director ordered it, and that he'd explain why when he sees me next week. How totally stupidly random is *that*?

And just when I was making lists of all kinds of Scientifically significant German words to put into this Letter to You too! Words like *Rassenhygiene* (racial hygiene) and *Minderwertigkeiten* (inferiorities) and *Krankheitsanlagen* (diseased traits), for instance. They're from the history of Social Darwinism, You know—the Applied Evolutionism that was so influential in certain circles in Germany not too long ago. I have to admit, just reading *auf Deutsch* about that little slice of Atheist history got me a little freaked on our behalf. Now I *totally* understand why *none* of us Brights ever mentions that history voluntarily! And to think about all those Atheist attacks on Pius XII, for what *he* supposedly did during World War II. Holy chutzpah!

Now back to what I was explaining. As if the Director in here isn't snarky enough, there are also the so-called attendants. Those guys—if they *are* guys; they're so metro I can't tell—freak me *totally*. They don't go around in those bright-colored scrubs like the orderlies

119

do in some regular old rehab, but in some kind of weird shimmery gray robes. And they don't wear those fake smiles all the time like orderlies and nurses do, either—You know, like the ones who come in chirping like, "Good *morning*, A.F. I think You'll be very *happy* with our crafts project today!" when the only thing I'd want out of that stupid crafts class is glue and lots of it, if You know what I mean.

No, the attendants in here don't act like anything like that. In fact, they don't even have real facial expressions. They're not happy. They're not sad. They just look totally alert. They're like that *New Yorker* cartoon of the tragedy mask and the comedy mask—You know, where they're both wearing the same exact look, and the caption just says "Botox"? Well, that's how these orderlies or nurses or whatever they are look too. There must be some stash of Botox in the Director's office, don't You think? If I weren't so busy writing these Letters to improve our new Atheism, I'd probably be wondering what else he has in there!

But now let's get back to our real reason for being here—Part Two of Your one and only Atheist conversion story! And no more digressions or little jokes this time, swear to Loser.

It's interesting, don't You think, given all the attention we Brights devote to the question of what draws the suckers to theism, that so *little* has been said about the opposite, that is, what might tempt people to Atheism? Oh, of course a handful of the Dulls—mostly the very worst backstabbing-enemy cranially supersized ones—*have* thought to address just this question of motive. I'm embarrassed to report, by the way, that their answers for why people turn to Atheism don't remotely line up with Yours. Not one of them seems to think that going godless has anything to do with succumbing to Reason and Logic, for example—not at all.

C. S. Lewis, for one, pulls the rug out from under us like this: "If you examined a hundred people who had lost their faith in Christianity, I wonder how many of them would turn out to have been reasoned out of it by honest argument? Do not most people simply drift away?" I can't pretend to statistical certainty here, and I hate to say the old Loserphile got anything right. But I'd have to say that based on what I've seen of most Brights I've known, he nailed that case shut.

Fulton Sheen—who incidentally gets under my epidermis like no other flack for Rome, though he also is mercifully as it were deceased—makes a different if also hateful point. He addresses what he calls the "anger" that colors so much Bright writing and thinking: "He who has fallen away from the spiritual order will hate it, because religion is the reminder of his guilt." Can You *believe* that guy? As if humorlessness and a low boiling point have anything to do with being drawn to godlessness! I got so mad when I read that one, I threw his book right across the room!

Yet Lewis and Sheen, much as I hate to admit it, get closer to the facts of my own personal conversion than any explanations offered by our own side. In the end, it was all very simple; and the simplest part of all went like this.

You see, if everything You guys and the rest of the Brights said is true; if we Humans really are just some tiny animate fungus on a somewhat larger rock of some kind, however statistically improbable, just orbiting one of those billions and billions of stars that Forebear Carl Sagan liked to talk about; if there really is nothing behind us and nothing ahead, nothing, *nothing, nothing, nothing at all*; if You guys and the other Atheists are right, and all Loser's poets, builders, painters, prophets, believers, and apologists stretching back over three millennia are wrong; if no one else really is watching us, or caring about any of us at all; well then, in this whole random cosmic rave of matter and antimatter, space and time, that just dwarfs every last thing any one of us will ever be or think or do—if *that's* really what we're talking about here, then *one* little elective medical procedure, one *teeny-tiny* exercise of a woman's right to choose by one *very* insignificant human female like A. F. Christian, shouldn't matter much to anyone, anywhere, ever at all.

Isn't that right, everybody? Isn't it just *right*?

Because that *is* how it all came down. We were living in Portland with friends by then, leechosaurus ex-boyfriend Lobo and I. His dad, as mentioned earlier, had finally kicked him out of the apartment in New York. Lobo managed to find a job at our nearest Starbucks, so he was actually working a little for once (though not much). I was sort of working too—not for real money, Loser knows, but just trying to get some of my fiction serialized online. But at least for the first few months there in Portland, things were more or less what You might call normal—or as close to that as two backsliding rehab regulars could get.

That's when I found out I was pregnant. And *that's* when Lobo, who is a hyper somewhat endorphically challenged head case even at his absolute *best*, which he rarely is anyway, really flipped out.

Now, inexplicably fond as I was of my hopeless ex-boyfriend—he wasn't all bad, You know, only mostly—I knew inside he did have a point. Bringing up a baby with *him*, I thought more than once, would be like giving someone a pig for a father (I don't mean that in the Peter Singer sense, of course).

But on the other hand, and even by that late date— months after I'd darkened any church doorstep, years after I'd really even talked to Loser—there was still enough of the former Christian left in me to put up some fight about it. We're supposed to be antiviolent, I told Lobo. We're *vegans*, for Loser's son's sake. We don't even kill the *roaches* in this place. And we're supposed to go and do something as unnatural and bloody and biologically imperialist as *that*? I probably said a lot of other things too, when I was trying to talk Lobo into keeping the baby; I'm trying not to think too much about that now.

But Lobo didn't want to hear any of it. Instead, he did what he always did when we fought and I won: stalked off to see his friend who ran the Internet café, and who was always on top of the latest Progressive stuff. And when Lobo finally came back that day, he had all Your books on Atheism and a bunch of others that his friend had loaned to him. He said they both thought I should read these books, because they'd prove to me once and for all that getting a You-know-what was no big deal.

So every day for a while, we took turns reading all those books on the new Atheism out loud to each other. And what with one crummy thing and another coming back to bite—I was throwing up like I was auditioning for the Ms. Bulimia contest, my sister texted me to say Mom was sick, our cable got shut off for nonpayment, and Lobo said the lights would be next—I started to weaken; and finally I caved. I went to Planned Parenthood and just did the thing, and then I went home as usual—home by then being defined as Lobo, Your books, some painkillers courtesy of PP, and lots of talk about how into all this new Atheism we both were getting.

The trouble was that despite my new belief system in all Your ideas, things started happening in my head and just wouldn't stop. First, I got this crazy but totally firm idea that the baby—as I could not stop thinking of it—would have been a girl. I'd see her if I closed my eyes—not looking like a tiny fetus and all, You know, but like a real little baby, all wrapped up in some little pink bunting and trying to curl her tiny fingers around mine. I started calling her H.D., Hypothetical Daughter, to myself. (You know H.D. already, I've mentioned her a couple times to You before.) And as time went on, I started to find myself talking to her more and more—and more.

I thought at the time that it was just some OCD kind of habit. Then Mom died unexpectedly a few weeks later, and the whirring and clicking inside kicked into overdrive. I hadn't seen her in a while, You see; she was not exactly approving of my current lifestyle. Somewhere deep in the cerebral cortex, I started thinking about them both together and couldn't stop. The most random ideas would come up, like, *If H.D. and Mom were both here today, I'd be seven months' pregnant and Mom would be visiting to help me get ready and doing stuff like making dinner for me.* Or, *In five years when I'm thirty, Mom and I will be going to see H.D.'s first kindergarten assembly.* Sometimes I'd tell Lobo about what was happening in my head, and he'd usually just hulk out on me. But that's just exactly what was happening, whether he went tattling to his friend at the Internet café about me or not.

The day I saw a doll on the street that was about the size of a human infant and brought it home and wrapped it up and sat it on the couch, Lobo finally went ballistic. That's when he went back to his friend and returned with those essays by fellow Brights that I talked about in the last Letter. "There!" Lobo said. "That all proves it! Because if even bestiality is okay, and if there's really no such thing as human dignity, and if even *infanticide* is getting a retooling, thanks to all our new Atheism, then what You did about that blob of cells has just *got* to be all right too!" And as I told You in the last Letter when we talked about the slippery slope, *this* time around, faced with all that incontrovertible evidence that the slope really did exist, I was just about certain he was right—at least about that.

But even so, I couldn't stop thinking. The day I set out a little tea party for Mom and H.D. to celebrate the doll's one-month birthday, Lobo finally packed up his junk and just left. I still don't know why. I even set a place for him at the table, like he even deserved it, which of course the slacker dirtbag totally *didn't*. I mean, the "birthday" cake wasn't even a real cake, just some stale old Little Debbie cookies, which were all that was left in the place. And we didn't even have real utensils that matched and weren't plastic, so I had to set the table with our little coke-cooking spoons. How lame is that for a one-month-old's party, anyway? I tried to explain how unfair he was being to both of them, but Lobo wouldn't listen. He just threw all his stuff into his duffel, grabbed whatever drugs he knew about that were lying around the place, called me a crazy you-know-what and a few other things, and off he went.

You know how some Humans morph into hypochondriacs and spend all their time online Google-searching diseases, convinced that they're going to find some obscure truth about what's malfunctioning inside them? That's how it was for me with our new Atheism, once Lobo left me alone with Mom and H.D. for good. All I did was read and take notes on Your books. *Somewhere* in there, I knew, I'd find the words to make me feel a little better. And the longer it went on, the more I understood that I really *did* have more invested in this new godlessness than anyone else did, and that I really *am* Your number one convert, bar none. That's why I started making those lists of all the factual errors and Logical problems that I talked about in the first seven

Letters, don't You see? I thought that if I could just make this new godlessness of ours airtight, Terminator bulletproof, and invulnerable to *any* question that *any* believer anywhere ever might hurl at it, I'd be off the hook I was on once and for all.

I was still working away at it two months ago, making my little notes and questions for You, when I looked at the calendar and realized that it was H.D.'s *actual* due date. So I celebrated the only way I knew how. First I went to my Facebook page and took down all the pictures of Lobo and me and replaced them with some pictures of the doll and changed my status to "single". I had to take a pass about dinner; there was nothing left, not even any of those Little Debbie cookies. Then I put the doll on my lap as usual, lined up every pill I could find in the place on the kitchen table, washed them all down with most of the last bottle of Grey Goose, and read some random old poem called "Mr. Flood's Party" to H.D. over and over again till I finally couldn't read anymore.

And that's really all I remember, until I woke up in this cuckoo-bird rehab place. There was some crack baby on the stretcher next to me, and the midget with the red cape was leaning over both of us not making a sound, and the weirdy attendants just took some kind of notes and stared with those crazy unblinking kind of eyes of theirs. Then they put me in a room somewhere with Rosetta German—and the rest of the story You already know.

Sorry if this Letter's been kind of a Debbie Downer, guys. But everybody wanted to know the real story of my turn to Atheism, and now You do! You can't say anything got left out *this* time, because it didn't! Besides, I'm personally sure that things are looking up! You know that song, "Hey There Delilah", that topped the music charts everywhere and won all those awards and how there's the famous story that the girl it was written for actually *dumped* the now totally famous guy who wrote it for her before it was released? Can You imagine what an idiot she feels like now? Well, that's how Lobo's going to feel someday, when he finds out about my Letters to all of You!

By the way, everybody, the Director told me this morning that I've got only one more week in this place, so we'll find out where they're transferring me next Friday. So that means there's only time for one more Letter to You about our divine godlessness. I'm going to make the most of it, guys! True dat! You'll be sooooo surprised and proud when You see!

> Yours more gratefully 4-ever than
> You will ever know,
> A. F. Christian

LETTER TEN
Onward, Anti-Christian Soldiers!
A. F. Christian Meets the Midget
in the Red Cape

Dearest Leading Atheist Saviors (as it were),

Major big day here in this funky psychobuggin' rehab place, guys! Today I'll finally meet with the Director and find out where they're sending me next!

Now on the one hand, I'm *totally* psyched about all that. There's nothing like that first day out of rehab to make You feel alive, know what I mean?! At the same time, I'm shaking just a little in my flip-flops. Do You think they're really going to let me go home (wherever that is now)? I'm not sure how. I haven't seen the outside of this place since I got here. I don't even know if they *have* one of those uh-oh buses for getting back and forth, like any normal rehab would have.

But never mind about what happens next, guys— we'll stress out about that later! The important fact for now is that since I *am* leaving one way or the other, this has to be my last Letter to You about our new Atheism. And it's one You really, truly need to read, even if it's a little long and You might want to print it for Your friends so nobody writes in complaining again because they missed certain plot details. It's about an absolutely *critical* subject—in fact, what for many of the believers is *the* most critical subject standing between us Brights and them.

Let me start by saying that I hope nobody got too bummed about my last Letter. I realize it was not exactly the most happy-bo-bappy story ever posted on the Web. But the thing is, I really had to go into all those details—You know, about Mom dying, and my dork ex-BF Lobo walking out on me, and how I had a You-know-what instead of having Hypothetical Daughter (H.D.), all within just a few months of each other. And I also had to fill You in on what happened next, i.e., my substance-laced "party of one" that last night in Portland, which is what landed me in this weird detox slammer or whatever it is that I am in.

Now, I wouldn't ordinarily go into all those personal details with some random bunch of guys on the Internet. But the reason I had to do it with You *particular* guys—i.e., You most popular Atheists on the whole planet—is because *exactly* that story brings me to the point of this last Letter. The problem for Atheism that my story illustrates ridiculously well goes like this: Why did I feel the way I felt in Portland about letting down Mom before she died? *Why* did I feel so totally hideous about what I did to H.D.? What's the meaning—or even just any plausible Natural purpose—of the human enigma called personal guilt?

I know what Your first thought is, of course! You want to explain that feeling of guilt away. You want to say it's just some vestigial adaptation that we Humans needed once and don't need anymore, like an appendix or a tailbone or a novel by Ayn Rand. But that kind of response just begs the question. The point here—as my own case goes to show, and plenty more starting with *A* for Augustine can too—is that this feeling of personal guilt can be highly destructive to a human organism. It's disadvantageous to human survival in the extreme. It's just not the sort of trait You'd expect to find in any creature who is *truly* ruled by selfish genes at all.

Okay, maybe You want to take some other tack—like saying I felt "guilt" because my mind had been poisoned by toxic Dull superstitions about how certain things are so-called sins, when in fact, as Science has shown, they're all perfectly fine. If only I had been as unflinching a Secularist as You, everybody might be thinking, I would have *understood* that a blob of cells has been firmly established to be no big deal—it's just a blob of cells and nothing more.

You could *say* all that—and if I had still been a practicing Dull, some of it might even have made sense. But again, the facts are otherwise. As I told everybody already, by the time I exercised my freedom of choice in Portland several months ago, it had actually been *years* since I'd been a Christian in anything but name only. Remember, I went all the way through a typical American college! Following which I spent two years shacked up with scumolicious Lobo, who was not exactly a poster person for Loser and his laws under *any* circumstances, let alone once we both got back into the sauce and the drugs.

I mean to say, by the time I went to Planned Parenthood that day, I was as empty of religious superstitions as any former believer can be. So why, again, did I feel as ripped up about what happened as I did? I mean, shouldn't Nature have designed me to be *happy* about getting rid of something that was going to interrupt my life? Wouldn't You think, given all our theories about survival, that a gene for putting nasty things behind You, and fast, would have been selected by now?

Why should I feel regret, if H.D. was only what You say she was? I don't cry when I get a pedicure! I don't go home and chop and snort a weeks' worth of Lobo's Ritalin prescription after I've just had a haircut! Just *look* at what happened to my measly little life—all because of that guilt over Mom and H.D. Do You know, I think I took so much stuff that last night in the apartment that I could have died? I get all shivery just *thinking* about that one. Because despite everything that's happened, and without even having a reason for it, I seriously don't want to die. I just wanted the remorse to stop.

Why, if evolutionism is right and Loser is wrong, should there be any place in the otherwise oh-so-sophisticated scheme of Natural Selection for a trait as useless and powerful and inefficient and self-destructive as human guilt? Nobody who's an Atheist talks about that, anywhere! And the problem is, guys, that while we Brights *don't*, the most strategically dangerous of Loser's heavier hitters *do*—because they totally get that the existence of shame and guilt does more to put people in touch with Loser than any other force.

Their idea, as our mortal enemy Phillip E. Johnson once put it, is that "the heartfelt admission that there is a moral law and that we have violated it is often the first step that brings the unbeliever to faith." They believe, along with another mortal enemy, Fulton Sheen (R.I.P.—not!), that "every man and woman alive experiences a sense of guilt when he breaks a natural law." The R.C.'s have whole centuries of brainos lined up who have done nothing *but* develop what they call this "natural law" stuff, starting somewhere around Paul and hitting a major leap with Aquinas and on into our own day with plenty of names You may not know but who, trust me, know all about Your ideas—in addition to Weigel and Novak and Neuhaus and some others I've mentioned, dangerous guys like J. Budziszewski and Robert George and Germain Grisez and more.

And it's not only the professional Christians who believe that guilt is inborn. Sheen, making the point that the experience of remorse is universal, quotes old Seneca saying that "every guilty person is his own hangman." He quotes Shakespeare going, "Conscience doth make cowards of us all." James Q. Wilson, who is probably the leading Social Scientist in America, wrote a whole book in 1993 on this same idea—that "we have a moral sense [and] most people rely on it even if intellectuals deny it." And this notion that there's an inborn moral code "written on the heart", in that traitor Paul's phrase, is *exactly* what leads many people to theism—because theism and theism alone accounts for the otherwise Evolutionarily preposterous fact of human guilt.

Now, You guys all know me by now! By zeroing in on this problem of natural law, I'm not saying our Movement isn't vulnerable on other fronts. That's why I wrote those first nine Letters, You know! As they all indicate, there are *plenty* of people out there taking issue with Atheism in other ways, and some of those treacherous

135

Loserites have synapses and neurons that fire at least as fast as Yours. If You ask me, given the sheer volume of complaints we're generating, we Brights need to get more strategic about our targets. How about jumping up and down on Kathryn Jean Lopez's Blackberry for starters! Every little bit will help, You know!

Now, I know from some of Your friends who've been writing me that some perfectly earnest nonbelievers don't approve of Your ferocity toward the Dulls. For those guys, godlessness is just part of the personal ecosystem they share with their peers—no more demanding than deciding between one recycled paper towel and another, say, or what to get from Netflix tonight. Furthermore, they don't think their Atheism has much downside. They don't think that by walking away from religion, they're going to jettison anything major that they might want back someday: morality, ethics, human dignity, that kind of thing. For reasons explained in Letter Eight, as You know, I think there's plenty of evidence that those nice-guy kind of Brights are wrong about that particular bet.

But whether they're easygoing Secularists or Dawkins-thumping major believers like You, militant Loser-haters or just fellow travelers, *nobody* out there on the godless team has answered the question in any way that makes Scientific sense: *Why do Humans feel shame and guilt in the first place?* And that failure, to be honest, has me very worried. I'm worried for our new Atheism, of course. But I'm also worried about me. Somewhere inside, I'm worried that something Michael Novak says in his horrible recent book, *No One Sees God: The Dark Night of Atheists and Believers*, might be true:

> I have come to understand what the Jewish Testament and the Christian Testament teach us about God, about human beings, and about ourselves is a truer account of reality than any other I have ever encountered. Much as my atheist friends will loathe it and mock it, I have tested this judgement in living and found it to ring true. It better meets the facts of my own reality, and the urgent inquiries of my own mind, and better turns aside thrusts intended to wound it and to destroy it, than any other account I have discovered.

That's what I'm afraid of, guys—that something like the Dulls' "natural law" does more to explain "the facts of my own reality" than anything I can find in all our godlessness. I don't want to up the ante on anyone, but I haven't much time left in here. If Atheism can't explain my feelings of guilt and remorse, which after all are the most powerful feelings I have, then I might have to go back to the side that does have an explanation for them—and I don't want that! Too much uncomfortable explaining to do there!

So *please* put on Your thinking caps, guys, and fast. I'm happy to be Your human guinea pig for some new Atheist explanation for guilt. (You know I don't mean that in a Peter Singer sense!) But can somebody please try and come up with something pronto?

One of those creepy gray-robed attendants is knocking now, so I guess it's time to go see the Director. Everybody cross Your fingers for me, okay? Don't worry—I'm still Your biggest fan ever! Nobody's more attached to this Atheism than I am, word, guys! Nobody, and I mean nobody, needs it more!

[*Editor's note: At this point there is a break in the Word document. The next keystroke occurs two hours later.*]

Dearest atheist brothers,

I know you won't believe these next few pages, and I probably wouldn't either if I hadn't been there. "Such secrets have been revealed to me that all I have written now appears of little value", as somebody you might want to read someday says somewhere. But I do want to get this all down before I go, because it's the craziest thing ever, and I know I'm going to want to remember it over and over! Even if nobody else out there does get it. Even if no one reads this but you.

So here's my story. When the freakazoid robotic attendant thing came to get me, he/she/it didn't take me straight to the Director's office like I expected. Instead, we went the other way—down to the ward where the crack babies are kept. At least I've always assumed they were crack babies, because I've never seen a rehab with as many infants as this one has. I had a spooky feeling all over just for starters. Then the attendant opened a door and brought me over to a crib and handed me—I am not making this up—a baby. And not some pathetic plastic doll like I found in Portland, either. I mean a real, breathing, pink baby in pink bunting, reaching out her teeny-tiny fingers for me.

So I asked the attendant, "How old is that baby?" and the thing said, "Two months exactly." Well, what are the chances of a coincidence like that?! You know that's exactly how old H.D. would have been now, if the due date was right. And I was just so blown away I couldn't believe it!

So I asked if I could just touch her fingers, and without saying anything the metro gray thingy put the baby in my arms. And of course I just bawled my eyes out like I was coming off my first binge! I kissed her little eyelids and played with her toes like a hundred times, and she did all the baby things that we're all "wired" to react to, just like you guys are always saying, cooing and smiling at me. She even patted my arm on the exact spot where there's a tattoo of Lobo's stupid name, you know, that he designed himself with a little green snake running through the two O's.

And I told her how sorry I was about everything, and she just sort of smiled some more and went Zzzzzz and Brrrr and whatever else random baby kind of noises. And all the while the attendant just stood there looking at us through those weirdy unblinking eyes they all have and didn't say a thing.

It was the freakiest moment ever! Because it seemed like it took forever and at the same time was over in a second, do you know what I mean? And I asked the attendant could I come back again and see the baby tomorrow, and he/she/it said it depends on what the Director says about where you're going next. And I said I don't care if I stay here forever as long as I can see her, because that's how I felt.

But after a while the gray thingy laid a hand on my shoulder, and I understood without its saying anything that I had to put the baby back. I must have been crying like it was raining in there, because I could feel that my whole face was soaking salty. Still, in we went to the midget Director's office anyway, and the attendant sort of swooshed me into a chair next to him and left.

The first thing the midget did, and it really surprised me, was to take the silky edge of his red cape and wipe my face. Then he told me not to be scared of anything, including him, and that he doesn't always look the way he does right now. He said that because of all the babies in this place, he makes himself into a midget when he's visiting them so he's more like their size and their level. He says he can do that, put

140

himself into whatever shape someone else needs, and apparently he can speak any language he wants too.

I know! I told you! How crazy was that—and just for starters! Sure, there's this midget who's got my life in his hands, drying my eyes with the hem of his red cape and telling me he's like some kind of alpha Animorph! Like I said, I wouldn't have believed any of it either two hours ago. But it's all true, and there's even more.

He asked me if I knew where I was, and I said sure, some kind of supersecure rehab. Then he asked if I'd ever read Dante, and I was kind of taken aback. I mean, it seemed so random! Now, it's true that I'd read plenty of Loser's apologists and quoted them to you guys, back when I was thought-stalking all their books in the effort to improve on your new Atheism. But Dante just seemed so fourteenth century I didn't think he even counted, know what I mean? I had the feeling the midget knew the answer already, but for some reason he wanted to hear it from me. Anyway, I told him no, I hadn't read Dante, and the midget just sort of nodded his head for a minute, then sat down close to me and took down his hood.

And that was like the freakiest thing of all, because I still couldn't see his face! In fact, I couldn't see anything at all—just light, light, and more light, in every direction I tried. But it wasn't light like we usually experience it; it felt liquid; only it wasn't exactly liquid either, because I could even breathe it too. It felt like the most wonderful thing that ever had gotten into my lungs (and in my case you know,

141

that's saying a lot!). Then the midget started to talk again, and this time when he talked it was just like when I was holding H.D.—I just wanted it to go on, and on, and never, ever come to a stop.

"You see, A.F.," he said, "this place you're calling rehab is kind of like House. *You like the television show* House, *my dear, isn't that right? And just like on the show, there are a bunch of really smart helpers in here—I call them the Messengers, though there are other names for them—and one of their main jobs is diagnosing the patients who come in.*

"Now, the Messengers aren't perfect," the midget continued— and here he gave some weird little snort—"and as a matter of fact, between you and me, A.F., some of them can be pretty obnoxious. But they are *quite knowledgeable about what goes on inside a person—far more knowledgeable than any of the patients here can be themselves.*

"And just as Dr. Gregory House's job on the show is to let his posse take the first crack at diagnosing everyone who comes in—because that's the only way they'll ever learn to get better at it—that's how it is with me and my posse too", the midget continued. "The Messengers go as far as they can and no farther. That's where I come in, just like House always does eventually—to explain what they've done right or wrong, and to figure out what the patient needs next.

"That's what happened in here in your case", the midget explained. "You showed up unexpectedly, and the Messengers had to decide what to do with you. And the most important

things they had to figure out were, did you feel remorse about what happened with H.D.? And did you really mean to check out for good that last night in Portland when you took all those drugs? Because everything *about what treatment you get next depends on those two things."*

As it turned out from the rest of what he told me, the Messengers had quite a fight over my case! (I told *you* I *didn't like some of those fey buggy two-faced little Kabuki posers!*) *And some of them said no, I didn't mean to leave Portland for good, and others said yes I did. Just like some of them said I didn't feel remorse about Mom and H.D., and some of them said yes I did too. So they talked it all over and finally took votes, and both times around the ones who were wrong won.*

That's why they gave me the Rosetta Stone German, the midget explained. It's because there are only two places where people can go from here, and in one of them—called Stalag Eins—*that's the only language anybody is allowed to speak. It was then that the midget stepped in. He suggested there was a better way for the Messengers to figure out what the truth was than taking votes on it. He said that if I wrote out all these Letters to you, they'd all be able to see* exactly *what I was thinking at the times in question. He said that after reading the first half of today's Letter—which apparently they did while I was holding that baby—they took* another *vote; and* this *time around, even the creepy, sneaky, metro backstabbing Messengers (my words, not the midget's) were unanimous about where I go next.*

Holy moly, guys—I can't believe the midget watches House! *Can you? But he sure seemed to know everything about it. He knows about lots of other random things too, as it turned out. He loves Johnny Cash, for instance. And guess what—I even asked him about the red cape and where he got it from! He gave a little laugh about that—he said nobody ever asked him before—and told me it was actually quite new. He saw one like it in a shop window in Rome that he liked, so he told some Polish friend of his named Karol. And when the Polish guy checked in here a couple years ago, he brought a red cape just like that with him for the midget! How cool is that?!*

Oh, and speaking of Italy, how cool is this: *the Director also told me that where* I'm *going next—someplace called* La Terza Sfera, *which he says is as far away from* Stalag Eins *as it's possible to get—they also speak only one language! And guess what: it's Italian! He gave me the Rosetta Stone kit for that, instead, as a good-bye present. Isn't that* awesome?

You say it's all absurd, I know. And it is! But compared to what? The idea that the chronological line from the lungfish, say, to a Bach sonata is somehow straight and self-evident? That a Shakespearean play really is just a matter of mathematical inevitability? That H.D. really was just a blob of cells? Or that the feeling that only grows in every man and woman as they get older, according to which their loves are infinite even as their time is increasingly finite, actually signifies nothing, nothing, nothing—nothing at all—despite the

144

fact that something deep down inside almost everybody says otherwise?

If it's any consolation, though, I really did enjoy writing those Letters to you all! I don't need them anymore, I guess, so they're yours to keep. Feel free to put them in the paperback editions of your books, everybody!

BTW, the Director also said that Mom and I—Mom!—could come here and get H.D. and take her back to our place for a tea party anytime we wanted to. He said we could have real cake too this time, because in La Terza Sfera they don't serve Little Debbie cookies. In fact, he said it would be the best cake I've ever tasted. And after everything I've seen, I believe Him.

No longer yours! Ciao ciao ragazzi (guys)!
A Christian

P.S. Even if we aren't BFF's anymore, could you guys do me one little favor? I mean, seriously, nobody's spent more time on your books than I have, and it's just a tiny thing!

If you see Lobo around anywhere, could you please tell him for me to stay away from his friend at the Internet café who gives him all those supposedly hot books and ideas? Because the Director told me he knows that guy too. It turns out he's only moonlighting there in Portland, you know. His real job is running Stalag Eins. How seriously stalking creeptastical not good is that!?

ACKNOWLEDGMENTS

Hearty thanks first and foremost to Kathryn Jean Lopez, the brains and soul behind *National Review* online. Without her decision to run the earlier version of this manuscript in online installments (thus making me finish it), *The Loser Letters* would not have become a book. Thanks also to the readers of *NRO* for their enthusiasm and helpful comments.

Special gratitude is also due to Fr. Fessio and the Ignatius Press team, whose confidence from day one has made the writer's yoke unusually light. Several friends likewise deserve thanks for their time and thoughts, especially Andrew and Denise Ferguson, P.J. and Tina O'Rourke, Stanley Kurtz, Tod and Tina Lindberg, Raphael Sagalyn, Joseph Bottum, and Michael Novak and his late wife Karen Novak. Thanks also to John Raisian, director of the Hoover Institution, for his abiding support of my work.

Thanks finally to my husband Nicholas Eberstadt, to whom this book is dedicated; to our children Frederick, Catherine, Isabel and Alexandra; and to their many teenaged friends whose cadences, energy, dramas, and Facebook pages have helped to breathe life into A.F. Christian. Only Loser, who has been thanked elsewhere, knows just how much.